Mysteries of the Life Force

Mysteries of the Life Force

My Apprenticeship with a Chi Kung Master

Peter Meech

SENTIENT PUBLICATIONS

First Sentient Publications edition 2007
Copyright © 2007 by Peter Meech

A paperback original

Cover design by Kim Johansen, Black Dog Design
Book design by Nicholas Cummings

Library of Congress Cataloging-in-Publication Data

Meech, Peter, [date]
 Mysteries of the life force : my apprenticeship with a Chi kung master / Peter Meech.
    p. cm.
 ISBN-13: 978-1-59181-055-1
 1. Qi gong—Ontario—Toronto—Anecdotes. 2. Qi (Chinese philosophy)—Anecdotes. 3. Vital force—Anecdotes. 4. Meech, Peter, [date] I. Title.

RA781.8.M44 2007
613.7'148—dc22

      2006029113

Printed in the United States of America

10 9 8 7 6 5 4 3 2

SENTIENT PUBLICATIONS
A Limited Liability Company
1113 Spruce Street
Boulder, CO 80302
www.sentientpublications.com

To my parents.

Contents

Dr. Chow and Peter Meech in Peter's 1955 Austin-Healey

Preface

There is much about chi kung that is extraordinary and much that defies common sense. Chi kung, variously spelled qi gong, chi gong, and chi gung, is an internal art devoted to the cultivation of chi, or the life force, and the life force, by its very nature, is remarkable and mysterious.No one knows exactly when the practice of chi kung began in China or what the first exercise or posture might have looked like. But whatever the form of its first manifestation, chi kung has evolved into thousands of different exercises and postures, all of them sharing one common purpose—the cultivation of chi, or the life force.

This book concerns events that took place during the first phase of my apprenticeship with Dr. Chow, a master of chi kung. The first phase began in 1985 and lasted seven years. Many memorable moments I have not included here. There were times he would make medicinal food for me, not because I needed it, but because I beseeched him for it—his Chinese food was the best I had ever tasted. There were times late at night when I would pass by the clinic, and I would see the light in his office turned on, and I would drop in, unannounced. At my urging he would push his paperwork aside and demonstrate, in the long shadows of the waiting room, various martial art forms he had mastered— Shaolin kung fu, Ba Gua, Hsing I—as well as other forms too obscure to be found in books. Sometimes he would dispel the loneliness of the night by telling me about strange phenomena in China he had heard about or witnessed first-hand. But these stories will have to wait for another time.

This book is neither scientific nor academic, but rather a first-person account of what it was like to study under the tutelege of a great master. If this account inspires others to study chi kung, then it will have served its purpose.

I sing the body electric.
—Walt Whitman

A Spy in the
Service of the Truth

Start with a whim, because that is how it starts.

I am resting in bed one warm spring evening when for no reason, just on a whim, I get to my feet, go to another room, and turn on the television. On the screen is an Asian doctor in a white lab coat making a series of rapid, artful movements with his hands. These movements he directs at a woman two feet away, and, behold, the invisible energy streaming from his fingertips turns the woman into a wind-up toy, her body shaking and jittering about.

The show is *Ripley's Believe It or Not*, and the narrator is Hollywood veteran Jack Palance. In his famous basso profundo, Palance explains that Dr. Chow is throwing healing energy called chi. As the segment ends, Palance lowers his voice to a dramatic whisper. Dr. Chow, he says, is a master of chi kung who practices this ancient art in Toronto's Chinatown.

I sit stock-still in a state of astonishment. Now whether this Dr. Chow is a healer or a hoaxer, I cannot say. But if he is a bona fide healer, I have just witnessed something extraordinary, something unexplained by science, something that a few centuries ago would have been called magic. I have always been fascinated with magic—not the stage variety, but the kind that becomes the science of the next century.

That night I turn over in my mind what I have seen. As an undergraduate I studied philosophy and religion and read widely in the fields of anthropology and parapsychology. In my mind, Dr. Chow's demonstration places him, if not squarely in the shamanism camp, then at least bivouacking on the outer fringes. But is he the genuine article, or merely a trickster?

For years I have been fascinated with shamans and sorcerers. I have been an avid reader of the works of Carlos Castaneda, a UCLA-trained anthropologist who wrote best-sellers describing his apprenticeship with a Yaqui Indian sorcerer named Don Juan. According to Castaneda, Don Juan was a man of power, someone who had extraordinary abilities that bordered on the supernatural. Critics have claimed Castaneda did his fieldwork in the deep stacks of the UCLA library, rather than rural Mexico and Arizona. The critics may be right, but Castaneda's stories of magic, whether plagiarized or actually experienced, have entranced me.

At first blush it would appear that Dr. Chow shares Don Juan's ability to manipulate energy in extraordinary ways. Dr. Chow resides not in Mexico, however, but in Toronto's Chinatown. And this fact is of particular significance to me, because I am currently living only half an hour away at my parents' house in a suburb of Toronto, having just returned from graduate studies at Stanford.

By the next day I have devised a plan. I will interview Dr. Chow for an article, and maybe, just maybe, in the course of interviewing him, I will discover the truth behind his paranormal abilities. To locate my subject I phone every acupuncture clinic in the phone book, but no one has ever heard of this Dr. Chow. Another flurry of phone calls, and I learn that *Ripley's Believe It or Not* is no longer in production; the episode I saw was over a year old. I am discouraged, but I mean to continue the search, though one thing is becoming clear: to hunt down the mysterious doctor will require sleuthing of a different order.

Strident Saturday. The entire Asian population of the world has descended upon Chinatown. Thumping rock music quickens the step of the thronging crowd. Against the side of a red-brick building I pause and wipe the back of my hand across my forehead. I am trying to find an herb store, an acupuncture clinic— any place with a connection to Chinese traditional medicine. As I move away from the building, I notice a large arrow, on which is hand-painted "Chinese Herbs." The tip of the arrow points down a flight of cement stairs, and so I walk down to a landing below street level.

Swinging open a heavy glass door, I hear a tinkling bell announce my presence, but no shopkeeper appears. As I move forward into the store, the contents of a long glass counter come into view. Exotic herbs, dried flowers, and strips of corrugated tree bark are crowding against velvety deer antlers and ginseng roots as large as a fist. I am perusing a tray of dried seahorses when, from behind the counter, up floats a cloud of thunderously dark hair. From inside this cloud peer two dark eyes, shielded by thick bifocals.

"Please?" asks the woman in accented English.

"I'm looking for a Dr. Chow. Do you know anyone by that name?" To this she makes no answer.

"I would like to meet him," I say.

Her eyes go inward behind the bifocals. "You patient?" she inquires doubtfully.

"Yes," I say without hesitation. "I am patient—a patient." The bifocals lower, and from under the counter appears a rotary phone. The woman dials a number with her middle finger, and then speaks into the receiver in short bursts of Chinese, tossing furtive glances in my direction. With a clatter the phone call terminates.

"You patient," she says with new-found conviction. "You go Beverly Street, one block. Go big house, left side." I thank her and bend my head once again to the marvels of the glass counter.

"You go now!" Her eyes widen with concern. "You patient!"

Big-house-left-side turns out to be a mansion of some antiquity. From a glance I can tell the stately dowager once housed a prominent family from another era, but the gradual encroachment of Chinatown has put the mansion under siege, and now the lawn has gone to crab grass, the white paint of the porch faded to a memory. Two raps and a heavy oak door opens, revealing a squat Asian man who appears to be waiting for me.

"First time apartment rental?" he asks, squinting with suspicion.

"I don't understand."

For my benefit he articulates each syllable: "First time a-part-ment rent-al?"

"I'm not here to rent an apartment," I say very slowly. "I'm here to see Dr. Chow."

After a moment's hesitation he retreats inside, leaving the door ajar. I blink away the streaming sunshine and stroll inside the foyer. The squat man has gone from sight, but another man has appeared in his place and is crossing towards me. He is a much younger, much larger man, with the slightly hunched shoulders of a tennis player and the weightless gait of a martial artist. His outsized hand swallows mine in a pumping handshake. "Dr. Chow's brother," he says in a high tenor voice.

At once I drop the ruse of being a patient and tell him about the article I want to write. Either he does not understand, or does not care, for a moment later he thrusts a sheet of ruled paper into my hand. "Name, birth date, phone number," he adds.

I look around for a place to write, and Dr. Chow's brother indicates an old phone booth that has taken up residence in a corner of the foyer. Sitting on the plastic seat inside the phone booth, I ponder whether the request for a birth date might be a nod to numerology. Who knows what ancient superstitions are practiced here? I finish writing and cast about for the brother, but he is nowhere to be seen. Waiting, waiting—is this some kind of supplicatory ritual the patient must endure before the great wizard grants him an audience?

My mind falls into a series of reminiscences about a certain wizard who captured my imagination as a child. Mr. Wizard was a character in a cartoon series. A reptile of indeterminate genus, his wardrobe consisted of a flowing robe and conical hat. His home was the hollow of a tree, his fan club, a young male turtle. The turtle wore a straw hat and starched white collar and lived in a shoe box. Each week the turtle would implore Mr. Wizard to give him a new life, a life where he could live out a fantasy career, be it as a sailor or knight-errant or some other unsuitable occupation. An exasperated Mr. Wizard would then wave a magic wand and send the hapless creature to his chosen destiny, and inevitably the turtle would get himself into a terrible fix. "Help me, Mr. Wizard!" he would cry out, whereupon Mr. Wizard would incant, in a thick German accent, "Drizzle drazzle drone, time for this vun to come home!" And through a spiraling vortex of primitive animation effects, the turtle would return back to safety. The turtle was a young male like me, but it was Mr. Wizard with whom I always identified. To be wise, to have in my possession a magic wand, to live in the hollow of a tree—this was the life to which I aspired. Is Dr. Chow another Mr. Wizard? In what secret hideaway is the doctor sequestered right now? The turtle never had to wait this long for Mr. Wizard to appear. Another ten minutes of perching on the hard plastic seat in the phone booth, and I get to my feet. *Drizzle, drazzle, dradle, drone. Time for this vun to come home.*

I am heading for the front door when, like an apparition, Dr. Chow's brother materializes from nowhere. He brings me to bay with a smile that stretches right across his face. "Sorry, Dr. Chow busy," he says. He takes the sheet of paper from my hand and lopes down a hallway, beckoning me to follow. We voyage to a large storage room at the back of the house where yellow light slants on a wooden floor through wooden shutters.

"Dr. Chow busy," he repeats. "But Jerry answer all question."

"Jerry?" I ask. With his head he gestures to a beige office-divider on the far side of the room. I turn to ask him who this Jerry is, but the brother has vanished. Tentatively I walk toward the divider and peer around. No wrinkled sage in full-lotus here, but instead a burly young man in black leather pants, sprawled out on an examining table. His shirt is wide open, and running down the center of his chest is a river of silver acupuncture needles. A black-visored motorcycle helmet rests on the chair beside him. Black mirrored sunglasses wrap around his face and submerge under a mop of black hair. As I step forward, his head rolls towards me, and his mouth opens. But instead of the gravelly timbre of a Hell's Angel, there comes a thin voice pitched to a high key.

"Why are you here this morning?" he asks. I tell him of my proposed article on Dr. Chow, but he interrupts. "Better watch out when you travel."

"I'm not sure I understand."

"I'm a psychic, so listen to what I have to say. You're going to travel to a third-world country, and better watch out because they're going to put you in jail." He gives himself over to a cough. "And furthermore—"

"Can we get back to Dr. Chow for a minute?"

But the psychic will not be deterred. "And furthermore, it will be several days before they let you out of jail."

The media theorist Marshall McLuhan once remarked that television was a cool medium—meaning that the viewer had to try hard to connect with it—but it is television that has put me in a storage room with a psychic telling me I will do time in a third-world jail.

"Hello, Jerry." I wheel around at the sound of the low voice. Dr. Chow is standing not three feet away in the open space of the door. Slenderly built, of medium height, he has a visible vitality —as if the atoms of his body were continually releasing small bursts of energy. He is wearing the same uniform from the television show: a white lab coat over a white shirt and nondescript tie. A thin black moustache, barely visible on television, is scattered above his lip. Gleaming black hair, barbered in a modish cut, falls half-way over his ears. It is hard to guess his age, but I put him in his early thirties.

"This writer over here," says Jerry, tilting his chin in my direction, "he wants to write an article about you. But that is not the real reason he is here. He will be your protégé, Dr. Chow. You will teach him." I flush with embarrassment and glance at Dr. Chow to gauge his reaction to this wild prognostication. He gazes at Jerry with Mandarin impassivity, and then slowly turns to me.

"Sorry," he says with apologetic firmness. "Too busy talk. Only have time for patient." He pivots around—head, torso, feet, in one stroke—then glides to the door like a ballroom dancer.

"When can I speak to you?" I call out. "For an article."

"Jerry answer all question," he says over his shoulder.

And like a puff of smoke the doctor is gone. On turning back to the all-knowing Jerry, I discover the question period has come to an end. The psychic has shut his eyes and is breathing heavily. Only for a moment am I idle before Dr. Chow's brother lopes back into the room. The next thing I know, I am standing outside the house with a piece of paper in my hand. The brother has slipped me the address of the new clinic, which is to open in a few weeks.

Youth is subject to wild enthusiasms that change from one week to the next. Two months after my visit to the clinic, I have completely forgotten about my desire to write an article about a

7

modern-day wizard. Instead, with all the resourcefulness of the indigent, I have managed to scrape together enough money to buy a plane ticket to India to visit a friend. Because of visa irregularities—meaning, I have no visa—I have been placed under airport arrest in Bombay. For the next five days my movements are restricted to a small waiting room. Airport arrest is not jail, of course, but in Bombay these distinctions are trifling. Two years later, under very different circumstances, I will have the occasion once again to meet Jerry the psychic, but that is getting ahead of my story.

Energy is eternal delight.
—William Blake

The Clinic

Back from India, my bank account drained to its last dollar, I get a job writing a screenplay, and I am thrilled beyond belief. As a graduate student I studied screenwriting, but this is the first time anyone has agreed to pay me to write a script. Despite my high spirits, my writing comes in fits and starts. In the last days of my travels in India I picked up a virus, and I haven't shaken it yet. During this period of half-work, half-convalescence, I move into a house with my brother and while unpacking some boxes, I come across the piece of paper with the address of Dr. Chow's new clinic.

I find The Canada Chi Kung Health Clinic in a row of two-story buildings tenanted mainly by discount stores and fast-food joints. Wedged between a diner and a Hair Salon, both hold-outs from the fifties, the clinic is an interloper from another culture, the bright red letters of the sign set toward the future. Covering the large plate-glass window are white gauze drapes, through which the waiting room is dimly visible. A door of tempered glass, set at an angle to the street, is the entrance. Opposite this door, embedded in the wall of the adjacent building, is a full-length mirror that must have once belonged to a tailor's shop. I glance at my reflection in the mirror—my face is drawn, my blond hair limp, my blue eyes lusterless. Dr. Chow will have his patient.

When the glass door shuts behind me, it makes a bang like a rifle-shot, but no one is around to hear. My eyes search the empty waiting room, which is an ode to seventies nostalgia with chairs of blue-cloth upholstery, a loveseat of canary vinyl, and a couch of milk chocolate naugahyde. Separating the waiting room from Dr. Chow's office are two oblong windows, obscured by more gauze drapery. I peer through the drapery to the office—empty. I cross to the admitting window; no one is there. Over to the French door that guards the hallway to the examining rooms. Through the panes of glass I see Dr. Chow and his brother leave one room and enter another. Neither man spares a glance in my direction, but wafting through the admitting window there now comes the sweet smell of burning herbs, and I breathe in the scent with pleasure.

I take a seat on the naugahyde couch. For some unknown reason the couch brings to mind the pop singer Barry Manilow, and quietly I begin humming a few bars of his syrupy anthem, "Looks Like We Made It." A sudden click of the French door, and Dr. Chow comes forward into the waiting room. A light appears in his eyes as he recognizes me, and I jump to my feet and make a movement to greet him. He keeps his distance, though, and we do not shake hands.

"Sorry. Too busy see you," he says in his low voice. "Another time." Without so much as a glance back, he swirls his white coat like a matador's cape and clicks the door shut behind him. No card, no phone number, no appointment for a visit. I hear another click; he has locked the door from the inside. Standing in the center of the tan all-weather carpet, I ponder my next move. On a side table there sits a rotary phone. Inspiration strikes, and on a piece of paper I jot down the number on the dial. As I leave the clinic, my mind is not on my sorry state of health, but on the phone. Just where does the Toronto Asian community get all their rotary phones?

A few days later I call the number. A voice, heavily accented, comes across the wire.

"Hello?"

"I'd like to make an appointment with Dr. Chow."

"Oh, this wrong phone," says the voice. "This only for patient want to call out."

"Yes, I understand, but I'm in need of medical assistance."

"Beg a pardon?"

It is then I utter two words of great magical power: "I patient."

"Oh, you patient! You come tomorrow, two o'clock! This Dr. Chow speaking!"

"And this is Peter Meech speaking. We met before, remember?"

"You patient now, so no problem."

I arrive at the clinic early, and after a few minutes Dr. Chow steps into the waiting room and gestures me to approach. "Come in, you patient now."

Inside his office I plunk myself down on a cushioned chair opposite his desk and let my eyes roam freely around the room. Copper plaques with engraved Chinese ideograms adorn the walls. On his desk sits a weathered Chinese-English dictionary, a Chinese newspaper and a stack of correspondence. To my left are glass cabinets filled with glass suction cups, boxes of acupuncture needles, and electronic machines I have never seen before. Beyond the cabinets is a private bathroom, accessible only through the office.

I ask the doctor where he studied Chinese medicine, and he replies that he studied at the Shanghai College of Traditional Chinese Medicine. But much of his knowledge, he says, he learned the old-fashioned way—from studying with different masters. I begin talking about his astonishing demonstration on TV, but he raises his hand for silence. Reaching over the desk, he takes my right wrist. "Check pulse."

Pressing his index, middle, and ring finger along my wrist, he feels my pulse—or *pulses* as I discover. He asks me how I am feeling, and as I recount my symptoms, he takes up a pen and scratches Chinese ideograms on a piece of paper. Then he feels the pulses in my wrist again, shaking his head. "Lung: 18%. Spleen: 25%. Digestion: 30%." Taking my left wrist, he gauges the percentages of my heart, liver, and kidney. More head shaking follows, and from this I infer I am a patient in extremis.

"How long have traditional doctors measured pulses?" I ask.

"Pulse diagnosis many thousand years old."

"When did they start measuring in percentages?"

He pauses and speaks with quiet modesty. "This method I develop from my own research." I ask what he would do if a patient had no arms on which to measure a pulse. "Measure pulse on foot," is his immediate reply.

"And if the patient had no arms or feet?"

"Measure pulse on throat."

"And if patient have—"

"No throat?" he says. "Then patient dead. No need measure pulse." A flash of amusement comes and goes on his face. Then he opens his mouth and sticks out his tongue like a panting dog. I give him a curious look, and then imitate him. He smiles with approval and writes down his diagnosis. With his head still lowered, he asks what I do for a living. I tell him I'm a writer, and he lifts his head and says, "Still want to write article?" I tell him I do, and he says I must take note of everything then, so I can record things accurately.

His attention lifts from me, and he directs his voice over my head. The next moment the tall brother pokes his smiling face in the doorway. I rise to my feet, and this time the brother claps my back with his huge hand, and in his high voice introduces himself as Alan. Down the carpeted hallway Alan buoyantly travels, with me, quite unbuoyantly,behind him. He then conducts me into one of the examining rooms.

At Alan's instructions I take off my shoes and socks, empty my pockets on a metal tray-table, and lie down on the examining table. Dr. Chow enters a moment later and regards with disdain the position of my splayed feet.

"Only dead people lie this way. You not dead...yet." Straightening my feet, he says, "Energy flow more smoothly now." He rolls up my pant legs and shirtsleeves. The gleaming cluster of needles in his hand makes my heart jump, and he says in a gentle voice, "Take deep breath."

In the space of a few seconds he inserts several of the hair-thin needles along my legs, arms and behind my neck. I ask how many acupuncture points there are in the human body, and he says there are over a thousand, with more being discovered each year. When I mention the slight discomfort of the needles, he gives a patronizing grin. For Western patients, he tells me, he inserts the needles only "little way."

To each needle, except the ones below my wrists, he attaches wires, and then he turns on a small machine that sends pulses of electrical current into my body. My legs, not used to the sensation, begin to jerk. Dr. Chow bursts into peals of high-pitched laughter, which brings Alan rushing inside.

"Perhaps the current is too strong," I say.

"No, is fine," replies Dr. Chow, and his body shakes with more hilarity, which causes Alan to explode with such a bout of laughter that he backs out of the room to contain himself. Dr. Chow, still smiling, drapes a sheet up to my chin against the coolness of the room. "Need rest," he says. As I shut my eyes, he turns off the overhead light and closes the door softly behind him.

Eventually my legs become accustomed to the current and twitch only slightly, but it is impossible to rest. Thirty minutes go by, and the doctor opens the door. He turns off the machine, plucks out the needles, and passes a pungent stick of burning herbs over the punctured points of my body. "Give moxibustion," he says, referring to the stick of herbs.

"What's moxibustion?" I ask.

"This I give you now," he answers

Back in the office he palpates my pulses once again. All of my organs have improved, but the state of my health is still precarious. As I leave the office, Alan hurries over with two bags of herbs. Elaborate instructions follow as to how to prepare the herbs, instructions that involve cooking, recooking, and cooking again, with different amounts of water being added each time. My head spins, and I ask Alan to repeat the instructions. In exasperation he gives the abridged version: "Cook! Drink! Repeat!"

That night I boil the herbs, which fumigates not only the kitchen, but the entire house. I raise a cup of the witch's brew to my mouth and brace myself for the first sip, but before a single drop has passed my lips, I begin to gag. It takes just over twenty minutes to down one small cup of the dark liquid between large mouthfuls of coffee Haagen-Dazs.

On my next clinic visit I complain about the taste of the medicine, and Dr. Chow says because Peter Meech is so ill, Peter Meech must drink the fourth level, or the worst-tasting herbs, which Asians themselves do not drink unless they have to. He has just discovered that my name is not Meech Peter, but Peter Meech, but still confuses his pronouns and a moment later blurts out, "When Peter Meech first come to clinic, she afraid have acupuncture!" He slaps the desk with merriment, rattling a long wooden case. My eyes fasten on the case, in which lie a pair of knitting needles, monstrously large, as if snatched from the nightmare of a child. Following the direction of my eyes, he picks up the knitting needles. "Special acupuncture needles. For you next time," he says in a quiet, uninflected voice. I jerk my head involuntarily. Laughing, he says, "No, this only for special illness."

"Where did you get them?"

"Upstairs."

"What's upstairs?"

"Oh, I live there," he says. "Alan live there too."

Weeks of ingesting fourth-level herbs and first-level Haagen-Dazs improves my health considerably, but I still have the occasional bout of asthma, a chronic condition I have suffered from all my life. In an effort to cure my asthma, Dr. Chow gives me acupuncture three times a week for the next two months and loads me up with bags of the detestable herbs. Twice a day I drink down the foul-tasting medicine and feel its strength entering my body.

Over time my asthma disappears. One day Dr. Chow checks my pulses, and something in the rhythm of my pulses appeases him. With panache he jots down the improved percentages of my organs and tells me they have climbed to almost 100%. He tents his fingers on the desk now and suggests I place an ad in the newspaper. I give him a quizzical look, and from a stack of papers he produces a local Chinese newspaper. Rifling to the back, he shows me several ads, placed by Chinese patients, singing the praises of their Chinese doctors. I tell him that because I am a Westerner I would rather promote his services by word-of-mouth—the Western way. He considers this for a moment before nodding his approval. On the edge of his desk I notice *A Visitor's Guide to Canada*, and I ask him when he first came here.

"1981," he says.

"Why did you choose Canada?"

"Norman Bethune," he says, raking a hand through his thick hair. "You know about this man?" I tell him Bethune was the Canadian doctor who spent the last two years of his life in China, attending to the sick on the battlefields when Mao Zedong was fighting the Japanese. I tell him Bethune introduced first aid, surgical techniques, and basic sanitation to China.

"That's right," Dr. Chow says with smiling eyes. He says he hopes to return the favor by introducing chi kung to Canada.

Chi kung! Over the course of my protracted treatment he had not mentioned it once. Chi kung! The word explodes in the air and sends a shockwave of delight through my body. I tell him I still want to write an article on chi kung. I ask what he can tell me about this internal art.

Dr. Chow bends forward now in the chair and speaks in a subdued voice. "I teach medical chi kung. Medical chi kung is soft chi kung. Soft chi kung build up internal body." For my edification he enumerates some of the benefits of medical chi kung: it prolongs a person's life by boosting the immune system and strengthening the internal organs; it enhances a person's creativity; it keeps a person young in body and spirit; it prevents senility; it increases sexual vigor; and it can aid in the development of psychic abilities.

He pulls on the lapels of his lab coat and says sagely, "If Peter want to learn about chi kung, should study chi kung." Study chi kung? Interviewing the doctor about chi kung and then writing an article—this I can manage. But *study* chi kung? As in learning by experience?

"Peter can learn better this way," he says, as if reading my thoughts.

"How long is this course?" I ask.

"Three times a week for three months." I hesitate for a moment and then surprise myself by announcing that I will do it; I will take the course.

"Any books you can recommend?" I ask. He shakes his head back and forth.

"Well, maybe I can find some books myself," I say.

"No read chi kung book," he says firmly. "This way, no can influence you." He swings his legs around and gets up quickly, and so I rise. But he signals me to sit down and carefully shuts the door. He returns to his chair and speaks in such a low voice that I shift my chair closer and ask him to repeat what he said.

"Must ask personal question," he says. "How many time a week, have sex?" The question freezes my tongue.

"Sex—how many time?" he repeats.

"I don't see what this has to do with chi kung."

His voice shifts, and he speaks with authority. "Tell you this—chi kung better than sex."

"Better than sex?"

"This I tell you."

He gets to his feet, and this time the meeting is over. Out the office and through the waiting room I stride, until I reach the entrance of the clinic. From the hallway comes his voice. "Just one minute!" He crosses the waiting room in a quick trot, nodding politely to a patient sitting in the corner. Sinking his voice below a whisper, he says: "One thing—no sex during chi kung course."

"No sex?"

"Energy need build up. Sex take energy out." He claps his hands to make the sound of energy leaving the body. The patient in the corner looks up suddenly, and Dr. Chow huddles closer to me, his breath light and sweet on my face.

"So, Peter agree, no sex during course?" He has a pen in his hand, and for a moment I think he wants me to sign a vow of celibacy. I imagine taking the statement to my lawyer for review.

"Peter agree?" he says again. I consider how three months and no sex might affect the relationship I began just six weeks earlier. It is not a contract to enter into lightly.

After a long pause I give my answer: "Peter agree."

At home that evening I speak to my girlfriend about the many benefits of chi kung, and she listens with rapt attention. Then I mention my three-month vow of celibacy, and an unpleasant grin appears on her face. She asks if I am trying to get rid of her, and I answer truthfully that I am not. Hours pass as she tries to persuade me to reconsider, but not for anything will I change my mind. By midnight the gleam has passed from her eye. Heading out the front door, she announces without looking back that our relationship is over.

The Sensual Nature of Knowledge

The first session. I empty my pockets of change and remove my watch. Dr. Chow has explained that during chi kung practice any metal on your person can take on an electric charge, absorbing energy that would otherwise move through your body. I climb onto the examining table, stretch out my limbs, and wait.

Dr. Chow whirls inside the room, takes my arms, which are folded across my chest, and gently places them by my side. Stepping back, he moves his eyes along the surface of my body as if tracing invisible lines of energy.

"One thing," he says in a deep baritone. "No misuse my chi."

"Misuse your chi?"

"Once have student misuse my chi, so take chi back. So give you this warning."

I ask myself how someone could misuse the doctor's chi. At this stage I can barely fathom how a person could *use* the doctor's chi, but Dr. Chow's prudential concern about his chi impresses me. He tells me to shut my eyes, and I do, thereby dashing any hopes of seeing him in action.

"How should I breathe?"

"Like bird fly and fish swim."

"And while I'm flying like a bird and swimming like a fish, what am I supposed to be doing?"

"Pay attention, and no fall asleep," he says.

"Pay attention to what?"

"To your body," he says. "And no talk anymore."

A few seconds pass, and then I hear the rustle of his sleeves. Is he moving his arms in the same corkscrew motion I saw on television? I keep my eyes shut, and when I open them, he has gone, and the room is in darkness. My attention shifts to my body where a tightness in my chest is causing me discomfort. Have I pulled a muscle? A sensation of heat begins in my sternum, and now a faint beating begins as if someone were tapping a finger in the small declivity. No, not a finger—a finger*nail*. The beating intensifies, taking on a sharp edge. It would be impossible to fall asleep with this sharp rhythmic beating. What am I to make of all this? Is this sensation the result of the doctor's chi? Or am I just imagining it? I do not think this is my imagination, but how would I know for sure?

Half an hour later there is a light knock on the door—the first of the thirty-six sessions is over. In the waiting room the doctor hands me a sheet of paper with a line of Chinese scrawled across the top. Underneath the scrawl I am obliged to record my impressions, a ritual I must complete after each session. As I begin writing, a sudden surge of energy moves across my breastbone, and I include this in my notes.

The second session. Dr. Chow performs his unseen gestures, leaves the examining room, and the sharp beating in my sternum resumes. This is not my imagination. This is real. Within ten minutes the sensation has grown stronger. I can endure it, but it is not altogether pleasant. Chi kung better than sex? You would have to be a masochist. My mind begins to wander, but the rhythmic beating—now a stabbing—recalls me to my body.

The stabbing chi leaves my sternum abruptly and draws a line to my abdomen, lodging about an inch and a half below my navel. There it remains for about a minute, before traveling back to my sternum. Back and forth, back and forth, back and forth. This I have not expected; this I have not visualized; this I have not desired. And yet the sensation is as real and palpable as if a sewing machine were deep-stitching a line up and down my stomach.

In his office Dr. Chow explains that the sternum acupoint I have discovered is the heart point, also known as the *shan chung* or the middle dan tian. The abdomen acupoint below my navel, he says, is known as the lower dan tian, or simply, the dan tian.

I am glad he did not tell me any of this earlier. Ignorant of the ways of chi kung, I am bypassing the filter of my mind and acquiring knowledge directly through my senses. I ask Dr. Chow about the function of the dan tian. The dan tian, Dr. Chow says, is the furnace of chi and one of its main storehouses.

As he speaks I glance at his folded hands, which, in repose, are undistinguished, the youthful skin stretched across ropes of tendons. The square fingers are of medium length; the spatulate nails pared down and etched with thin white lines. Who would ever suspect these ordinary fingers could wield such prodigious energy?

The third session. Dr. Chow interlaces his strong fingers on his desk and gazes at me from under his dark brows.

"What you do last night?" he asks.

"Nothing," I say, surprised at the accusatory tone that has crept into his voice.

"You do something last night." It is a charge sprung on the spur of the moment, and I look at him with incomprehension, trying to extract a meaning from his face.

"What you do?" he repeats.

I have no confession to stammer forth and shake my head left and right. "Nothing."

His bright dark eyes search my face for an answer. "What you *do?*"

"Went to a party, came home, went to sleep. Nothing."

"Ah!" he slaps the desk with his open palm. "What happen at party?"

"Ate something, talked to some friends, danced with an old girlfriend."

"This dance! How long it take?"

"How long? Ten minutes maybe." His body tilts closer, and the clear current from his eyes grows stronger. "And you dance together?" he asks. "You do this?"

Leagued with the Devil himself, I confess to my evil doings. "We danced together, yes."

Up flies his hand. "All my patient I tell them no sex during chi kung! For you, no sex and no dancing! For you, dancing just like sex!" He bounces a little in his chair and dabs his forefinger at me, his voice leaping up an octave. "You pass all my chi to this girl! Waste my energy! Do again, you out of the clinic! Now must build you up from beginning!" I stare at him in disbelief.

"Go to your room!" he says. Like a chastised child, I rise obe-diently, and only then do I realize he means I should go to one of the examining rooms.

Lying on the examining table, I review the conversation in my mind. The notion that one individual can diminish the life force of another is something I have recently been considering. For the last few weeks I have been writing for a Robert Halmi television show called *Dracula: The Series*. In each episode the young heroes struggle to prevent vampires from stealing the life force of human beings. I speculate that in the real world people who are low on energy might unwittingly become energy vampires, sucking the life force from those around them. And it makes sense that those who have a surfeit of energy might unwittingly give it away. As I lie on the examining table, I consider how odd it is that probing the Dracula myth should help clarify one of the mysteries of chi transference.

My ruminations are cut short when Dr. Chow breezes into the room. Anticipating his chi transmission, I shut my eyes, and a moment later I hear his arms slice angrily through the air. His breath goes out sharply. Then the door clicks shut behind him, and his footsteps recede down the hallway.

Panic...I watch for the familiar beating in my sternum, but there is none. Fugitive thoughts race through my brain. Maybe this time he did not throw any chi. Maybe this is a test to see if Peter really feels chi at all, or if Peter just imagines chi. Or maybe—maybe he snatched back all of his chi as he did with his other wayward student. Defeat...Fifteen minutes into the session, and there is no feeling whatsoever. I open my eyes and stare at the dark ceiling. So it is true—without knowing it, I have betrayed the doctor's trust. I have misused his chi. Hope...Twenty minutes into the session a beating begins in my sternum. But the beating is faint, and the session ends with no sensation of any kind registering in my dan tian.

On the couch in the waiting room I write a scant few sentences about the session. In an act of clemency Dr. Chow gently takes the sheet of paper from my hand, and when I look up, his glance falls upon mine with kindness.

"No stay up too late, no exercise too much, no worry too much. Lose chi this way." As a further precaution he advises I avoid physical contact.

"What about a handshake?" I ask him. "People like to shake hands in this town."

"Handshake," he says with a laugh. "What can you do?" So at least shaking hands is a pardonable use of chi, I think to myself.

Chi alert as I leave the clinic, and a woman carrying two large packages jostles me on the sidewalk, jostling chi from my body. Chi alert at lunch as a fellow writer greets me with the suf-focating hug of a returning sailor, and I drop another pint. Chi alert as a female friend comes over to my table and leans forward to plant a kiss on my cheek. Involuntarily I recoil, and she laughs, thinking she has caught me off balance. But I am off balance. I am the Boy in the Chi Kung Bubble. Smile at me if you will, talk to me if you please, but keep your hands away from my chi.

*Can you let your chi develop until it
becomes as supple as a newborn child's?*

—*Tao Te Ching*

The Nature of Chi

"How does the chi know where to go?"

Dr. Chow smiles enigmatically. "Chi know."

I hand over the description of my tenth chi kung session. My notes describe how the pulsing energy has traced a line from my abdomen to my groin, surged under my torso, and climbed to my lower back.

"But how does it know? Do you send the chi to a specific place?"

"Because I am doctor, I know which chi kung point need energy. Chi go where I throw it. Then after, chi go where it want." He flutters his hand to indicate the vagabond nature of the mysterious energy. I understand the concept of throwing chi to a specific point in the body, but I still do not understand how the chi knows where to go afterward. I ask Dr. Chow if the body leads the chi along certain meridian lines. "Chi know where to go by itself," he says.

"So this is not a form of body wisdom?"

"This chi wisdom," he says.

"But how does the chi know where to go?"

"This the great mystery of chi. Can also say this the nature of chi."

In the next session a cauldron of chi heats up my dan tian. Back in the office, I tell Dr. Chow of another sensation—wind blowing across the crown of my head. He raises his nose, his eyebrows, the evanescent lines of his forehead.

"Chi leave your head through the *bai hui* point," he says. I feel a measure of accomplishment until he adds, "Your body not strong enough to hold my chi. So my chi fly out."

More sessions follow, and the wiring of my body improves to the point where the chi is no longer exiting my head. Instead it scoops around the lower part of my torso and burrows into my lower back, at a point opposite the dan tian. Heat accompanies this burrowing, and later in the office I ask Dr. Chow what this means. He explains that the the *ming men* point—the "life gateway"—has been activated. Between the dan tian and the ming men, he says, there is an invisible cord of energy that passes right through the body.

The chi does not remain in my ming men point for long. The next session it breaks loose and clambers ever so slowly up my spine to a point just below my shoulder blades. The plodding, itching energy makes me want to scratch. But touching an area where chi is moving, I am told, can deflect it from its natural course as the fingers absorb the energy. The chi in my back feels slightly uncomfortable—as if a gigantic centipede with hot foot pads were creeping up my spine.

Below my shoulder blades there is an invisible barrier that the centipede cannot cross, and the feet stamp angrily in place before abandoning the ascent and pitter-pattering back to my tailbone. With two more sessions the centipede is able to climb one vertebrae higher, but the barrier still holds, and the centipede retreats once more.

From earlier readings in kundalini yoga, I recall that the serpent energy travels up the spine and over the head, coming to rest at the third eye. Surely this ancient pathway must be the one that the chi is forging in my body. But what a difference there is between reading about the kundalini energy and experiencing it! Bertrand Russell correctly identified the yawning gulf that exists between knowledge by description and knowledge by acquaintance. Experience has no substitute.

Another session comes and goes, and the rising chi stalls once more at the level of my shoulder blades. Then one afternoon, as I record the details of my latest session, a dashing young man emerges from the hallway and crosses over to the couch where I am seated. Sheldon is a real estate agent and the youngest of the three Chow brothers. I peg him as mid-twenties, but later I will discover that his youthful good looks owe more to his ardent chi kung practice than genetic good fortune.

When I tell Sheldon about the impasse at my shoulder blades, he smiles, dimpling his cheeks, then reaches behind my back and drags his finger up my spine. Immediately the chi shoots up my back, bursting past my shoulder blades like fireworks and burning a pathway to the nape of my neck where its journey ends with a steady pulse. With ecstatic surprise I describe the new trajectory in my notes. When I relay the latest development to Dr. Chow in his office, he listens with approving eyes.

"But why do I have such an intense pressure in the nape of my neck?" I ask.

He crooks his forefinger inside his thumb, making a tiny circle. "This *da zhui* point, very narrow. Difficult for chi to pass."

"Sheldon helped me open this point."

"Sheldon have good kung fu," he says with a smile.

"Kung fu?"

"This mean Sheldon have good skill, good technique."

During the next session the chi travels up my back to the da zhui point in my neck, but it tarries only a moment before climbing up the back of my head and flowing like a many-branched river across my scalp. At the top of my forehead, the chi sluices in one narrow channel, dropping to the area between my eyebrows, known colloquially as the third eye, or the upper dan tian. There the chi rests, beating a steady tattoo. At last! The chi has followed along the route described by the ancient yogis, a route that most Western scholars assumed was a metaphor for spiritual transformation, something to be visualized, perhaps, but not sensually experienced. In Buddhist terminology the third eye is known as the area of curled white hair. According to legend, when the Buddha became enlightened, the space between his eyebrows shed a white light. I am far from enlightened—my third eye has not opened. From the hidden eyelid, there is not even a flutter. And yet, the chi has undeniably set its tent here and hammered in its stakes.

Another session sends the chi off to traverse its usual course, beginning in my abdomen and circling around to my third eye. But as I focus on the beating third eye, an extraordinary thing happens. The chi slides down my nose, tickles my nostrils, cascades down my chin, and plunges down my throat where it slides to a halt at my collarbone. A sensation both novel and thrilling, it feels as if someone has stroked my face and throat with the soft tip of a feather whose shaft is plugged into an electrical outlet. I rush into Dr. Chow's office and tell him of my experience.

"This path very old, very important," he says. I am cheered and made strong.

"Where does it lead?" I ask. He utters not a word and allows no expression to be read on his face. My eyes venture to the top of a cabinet where stands a tiny naked man made of rubber. Crisscrossing the rubber man's body is a patchwork of colored meridian lines—the energy pathways of acupuncture. Dr. Chow leaps to his feet and makes a screen with his hands in front of the rubber man.

"No, must find out for yourself."

I find out the very next session. The chi begins in my dan tian and circles around my torso until it comes to a standstill at my collarbone, Then, with sudden explosive force it erupts down the front of my chest to the *shan chung* point in my sternum where it hesitates for only a moment before flowing back to my dan tian. And still it keeps moving, snaking downward and scooping under my torso to my lower back where it begins the ascent of my shoulder blades once again. For half an hour the chi purls around my body—a stream of rippling energy. For half an hour my body is a priesthood of one, consecrated to the moving daemon within. Without knowing it, I have taken a journey backward in time, back to first things, back to a primitive energy system the human race has long forgotten. Circulating in my body is something ancient and venerable, the elixir of immortality, Ponce de Leon's fountain of youth.

When I write down my impressions in the waiting room, I remember something Thoreau once said. The Northwest Passage, he said, is not what we should expend our energy to find. Instead, we should discover continents within ourselves. Of course, Thoreau was speaking of psychological continents, but what of the physical continents within ourselves? What of the rivers of energy that traverse those continents?

Dr. Chow supplies the ancient terminology for the riverine pathways traversed by this life-giving force. The chi flows down the front of my body, known as the conception vessel or the *ren mei* or *ren* channel, and it climbs up the center of my back, known as the governing vessel or the *du mei* or *du* channel. He tells me the small circle is the basic energy circuit in chi kung, also called the microcosmic cycle, or the Small Heavenly Orbit. I tell him I prefer to call it the Small Heavenly Orbit, for when the chi orbits around my body, my whole being floods with ecstasy, and I am in heaven.

The Large Heavenly Orbit

When I was four years old, I knew with a child's impenetrable logic that it would be exciting to hurl myself, headfirst, through the glass panel of our screen door. Someone about to leave the house? I would rush to the hallway and sprawl on the tile floor where I would listen for the door's asthmatic wheeze, so similar to the wheeze I carried in my lungs almost every day.

The clack-clack-clack of black Oxfords—my older sister is approaching! Her hand grips the door handle! The door is opening! I spring to my feet and assume the stance of a runner. My sister steps outside, and I run—barefoot—across twenty squares of tile. And just as the door wheezes shut, I dive through the lower glass panel, rolling onto the cement stoop. From the kitchen my mother hears the sound of breaking glass and rushes to the door, wiping her hands on her green apron. She finds me on the stoop, unmarked and smiling, brushing large glass splinters from my hair like Superboy. I tell her that diving through the glass was the best feeling I've ever had and can I please do it again.

And now I am in a chi kung clinic, feeling the same thrill of diving through a glass door every time the small circle activates in my body. Dr. Chow says he is delighted by my progress. He is standing in a shaft of light as I lie in semi-darkness on the examining table. I ask him if it is traditional in China for a master to give so much chi to a student, and he tells me that masters in China almost never give their chi away. They have worked hard to obtain their own chi, he says, and they naturally want to keep it for themselves.

Telling me to close my eyes, he moves farther into the room. I hear the rustle of his sleeved arms, and in my imagination I see his arms making graceful arabesques in the air. A moment passes, and I feel a sudden tingling in my abdomen, but I say nothing. The door shuts quietly, and for the remainder of the session the chi diagrams the small circle in my body, but this time I also feel the chi dappling my cheeks and dancing around the rims of my ears.

A loud noise erupts in the hallway—glass crashing inside a box—and my body jerks. A moment later, Dr. Chow charges inside the room and runs his hands a few inches above my torso, as if smoothing down a bed sheet.

"What's wrong?" I ask.

"Noise in hallway," he says softly. "Noise get your chi stuck."

"Did you fix it? Did you fix my chi?"

"Did. And give you more."

He leaves the room, and immediately I feel the chi thumping in my dan tian.. The sensation is startling, but no more so than Dr. Chow's demonstrated ability. I think about the Indian gurus who grant *shaktipat*—small bursts of energy—to their favored disciples. The disciples regard this energy as a sacrament and their gurus as gods, and yet here is Dr. Chow, with no claim to religious authority, dispensing chi to any number of students and patients on a daily basis. How can it be that he has such vast reserves of energy?

With more sessions the chi continues to deepen the groove of the small circle, and one day I feel a burning sensation in the center of my palms, and then my left wrist, which I broke as a child, begins to ache. Next my right ankle, never fully healed after several sprains, begins to twinge with a sharp pain. And suddenly my head feels like it will implode. I am no longer in heaven, not even floating on the clouds. I am back on earth, beset by earth-bound tribulations as the chi mounts a siege against my body.

Back in the office, Dr. Chow says the chi is healing old injuries and clearing away energy blockages. I should expect the painful process to continue for a while, he says. When I ask how long is a while, he stares at me with his dark round eyes. "Depend on your body."

I have been reading a biography of Krishnamurti, perhaps the most revolutionary religious thinker of the 20th century. He believed that an intelligent energy had cleansed his body. "The process," as he called it, continued for years. Of course, it is quite possible that his process was of an entirely different nature than my own. I certainly hope so.

For weeks I watch my body with a fascinated dread as it undergoes a deepening purge. Then one day, during a session, the pain stops abruptly. And just as suddenly the chi begins to spread—and spread ravenously. After completing most of the small circle, the chi deviates at my shoulder blades and traverses down my arms to my hands, making my fingertips tingle. Tripping up the inside of my arms a second later, it moves to the midpoint of my collarbone and then drops to my dan tian—pulsing, pulsing—and with a whoosh, rushes down the outside of my legs, all the way to the soles of my feet. Reversing course immediately, the chi shoots up the inside of my legs. Like a microbial creature endlessly multiplying, the chi insinuates itself throughout my body until every cell seems to tingle with new energy. I follow the chi as it moves further and further inward, to a place where it mingles with the very wilderness of my being, timeless and separate from everything I know.

A light knock on the door returns me too soon to the darkness of the room, and I open my eyes, blinking at the slit of yellow

light that lines the door's edge. In his office Dr. Chow congratulates me on discovering the large circle or Grand Heavenly
Circulation. He explains that the acupoints in the middle of the
feet are known as the *yong quan* or bubbling springs; and the
points in the middle of my palms are the *lao gong*. He says there
are eight extraordinary channels in the body that act like reservoirs of chi for the twelve meridians. Practicing the large circle
means that these reservoirs are full of chi and that chi is flowing
freely through my body.

I ask him how long it would take to achieve the small circle
on one's own. In China, the doctor tells me, one traditionally
studied chi kung under the guidance of a teacher and would typ-
ically reach a small level of success—completing the small circle—in three years. Reaching a big level of success—completing
the large circle—would take nine years, but only if one's body
was capable of completing the big circle at all. I have a sudden
intuition, and I ask if he achieved the small circle at an early age.
He nods with a bright eye, but gives no further answer.

"Does everyone who takes the three-month course have the
same experience?" I ask.

"Most have same result," he says, "but chi always move little
different with each person."

In rare cases, he explains, the chi will complete the small circle in the reverse direction—up the front of the body and down
the back—and no one knows why. Most of the time, he says, chi
will circulate more readily in the arms than in the legs. As evidence of this, he points out that people in the healing arts circulate chi to their hands on a regular basis, though they have not
completed either the small or large circles.

I ask him if any of his students have had poor results. He
reflects for a moment before answering. A few students, he says,
did not store up their surplus energy, but invested it in their jobs
instead, working longer hours and sacrificing sleep. In China, he

says, chi kung was not taught to people who were in business, because a stressful life makes accumulating chi very difficult.

As he talks, I feel chi moving around my dan tian, but I have not seen him throw it. Am I imagining this? Or am I warming myself against the calories of heat given off by his body? I want to ask him what is happening, but he swings his eyes toward the door, and a look of abstraction comes over his face The conversation has come to an end.

I have completed the last session, and Dr. Chow now guides me by the elbow to the entrance of the clinic and counsels me to practice every night before I go to bed and every morning when I rise. Practicing means relaxing and allowing the chi to flow where it may. I thank him for everything and grab his hand to shake it goodbye. His hand is surprisingly cool to the touch—as if he has granted it only the minimal amount of blood necessary to flex his fingers. The next morning I lie in bed for an hour before getting up. Pure delight as the chi scatters to my face, my arms, my legs. I consider that if the root of the word religion comes from the Latin *religere*—to ponder, take account of, observe—and if the object of observation is something one is in awe of, then observing one's chi could be considered a kind of religious act. The more I observe my chi, the more I am brought back to a fascination with the natural world, with my own body, with the riddle of creation.

The Call

To strengthen the large and small circles I embark on another course of study with Dr. Chow. Within the first few sessions, the chi's meanderings become as natural as breathing. On two occasions I fall asleep on the examining table, and Dr. Chow scolds me after reading my confessional. I must stay awake, he says. Focusing on the chi, he says, increases its power.

The statement gives me pause. If focusing my mind on the chi can change the chi materially, then my consciousness is affecting matter—if chi can be deemed matter. I consider whether there could be an analogy to the observer effect in physics. According to modern physics, the very act of observing an atomic or subatomic particle changes the physical property of that particle. If you measure the location of an electron, you cannot measure the momentum. If you measure the momentum, the location is lost.

Measure chi with the mind, and the chi grows stronger. I have also recently discovered that I can change the chi's location by shifting my attention to another part of my body. The chi may be in my hand, but if I shift my focus to my foot, it moves there as well.

After a few more sessions of lying on the examining table, the lazy man's way to health and happiness draws to a close. Now Dr. Chow instructs me on how to perform sitting chi kung, the next rung up on the chi kung ladder. In this variant, the practitioner sits on a chair with the hands resting comfortably on the knees and with the legs shoulder-width apart. The spine is kept straight to minimize the loss of chi to the chair, and the clothing needs to be loose, to permit easy passage of the chi along the surface of the body.

Over time the new position pays dividends as new and varied sensations appear. One day I experience a chi beard—with the chi hanging from my chin like a strip of molasses. Another day a conga line of ants is moving around my waist, tracing a line that I later learn is the *dai mai* or belt channel, which serves to regulate the gall bladder. Once in a while I contract a chi headache—similar to what I have experienced in the supine position, but more pronounced. When I look in the mirror, I notice my skin is healthier. Where blood goes, chi goes, Dr. Chow explains, so the chi is reaching every cell of my body.

Three months later, I finish the last session of the second course. Dr. Chow walks me to the door and drops a hand on my shoulder, not ungently. In a soft voice he reminds me to keep practicing. The next morning I consider calling the clinic and signing up again, but this time I think better of it. If I can so easily generate both circles on my own, why embark on another course?

But Dr. Chow is not without a Meech for long. My brother has let his curiosity about Chinese medicine get the better of him, and Richard registers first as Dr. Chow's patient and then as a chi kung student. His first session is nothing less than astonishing.

Swiftly the chi ignites his dan tian, then flames of chi lick at the base of his spine, then the lao gong points in the center of his palms begin to pulse.

My brother is a natural, and Dr. Chow is so impressed with Richard's ability that he wants to train him alongside me. Two brothers, he explains, can engage in a peaceful competition that can spur both of us on to greater heights. It's an intriguing idea, but I have decided not to continue the training, and I convey this news to Dr. Chow through his new emissary. Richard graduates his course with flying colors and quickly enrolls in another. But he is coproducing *Millenium: Tribal Wisdom and the Modern World*, a ten-part documentary series, and his work will take him around the world, preventing him from studying further. One day, before leaving the country, Richard returns from the clinic with a message.

"Dr. Chow wants to see you again." Then in a perfect caricature of the doctor: "Tell Peter Meech come visit. Need study more."

"Please tell the good doctor I appreciate his interest in my welfare, but I'm satisfied with the level of my practice." I explain further that I have been practicing diligently on my own, and on occasion have experienced chi moving in my body without any effort at all. So why do I need more instruction?

That night I have a dream about the doctor, which I dimly remember as one long conversation. With the first freshness of the day, the words and images flee, but my psyche is altered in a way I cannot explain, and a plan rises fully formed in my mind. A few hours later I sail like a freshly painted pinnace into the clinic. Dr. Chow greets me at the office door and samples my hand. He's checking my meridians, I think to myself. But he says nothing until we move into his office where he palpates my pulses at his desk. To my relief, my percentages are down only slightly. He asks what my symptoms are, and I tell him I have none. The reason for my visit, I explain, is to present a proposal—I would like to offer a lump-sum payment to study chi kung for the rest of my life.

He throws himself back in his chair, and his eyes close slightly as he focuses on a space above my head. This he has done before, and it always feels as if he were measuring me by his own mysterious standards.

"If you agree," I say, "this means I can study chi kung five days a week if I want."

He brings his body forward suddenly and places both hands firmly on the desk. "Peter go inside, do chi kung."

"And the lump-sum payment?" I ask.

"I think about it," he answers, his face an expressionless mask.

I go to one of the rooms and begin practicing the sitting position. Immediately I notice something different about my practice. In substance the chi seems thicker and hotter, and the more it circulates, the heavier my body becomes until I feel as if the ponderous weight of my limbs could crack the chair apart at any moment. It is with difficulty that I rouse myself to my feet at the end of the session. In the waiting room I write down my session notes and when I read them to Dr. Chow in his office, he smiles with bright comprehending eyes.

"When feel this heavy, three men can't lift you. Chi go deep into the ground, like roots of a tree."

My body is still flushed with heat when I prepare to leave the clinic. My jacket I have draped over my arm; my baseball cap is clutched in my hand. Dr. Chow sees me from the hallway and calls out.

"Must dress warmly. Cold outside."

"But I'm hot right now."

He crosses over and lowers his voice. "Doesn't matter. After practice chi kung, all pores in your body open. So easy for cold and wind get inside." I tell him I have seen him outside the clinic in the extreme cold in nothing more than a long-sleeved shirt. "Advanced chi kung, this different," he says. "No worry cold." As I don my jacket and cap, I ask him what he thinks about my earlier offer. "Still think about it," he says.

A month comes and goes. I am practicing chi kung every day now, and still I have not paid a nickel for the new instruction. Again I ask if he will consider a lump-sum payment.

"Still think about it," he responds.

Dr. Chow is according me special treatment, and I have no idea why. I begin to suspect he has taken me on as an apprentice of sorts, but there has been no discussion on this point. So what is really going on? The answer comes from a psychic,not Jerry the psychic,but someone I have never met—and will never meet—on the other side of the world.

I am helping Dr. Chow unpack some boxes of herbs in his basement when he tells me a story. There was a psychic who lived in a small village outside Shanghai, and Dr. Chow was curious to meet him. He took a bus to the village and then walked to the house where the psychic lived. In the fashion of a true story-teller, Dr. Chow now imitates the manner, voice, and appearance of the psychic. Rolling his eyes into the back of his head, he thrusts his hands out searchingly into the air. Evidently the psychic was blind.

"Welcome to my house," says Dr. Chow in the quavering voice of the blind psychic. He says he told the psychic his birth date, nothing more.

"And what did the psychic say in return?" I ask.

"You doctor," says Dr. Chow, imitating the psychic again. "And you live in the south. But you will work in the north on the opposite side of the earth."

Dr. Chow opens his eyes and offers his commentary. "First thing, he say that I doctor. How he know this? Then he say I live in the south—this true—that I will work in the north, but not in

China, in another country. How he know this? No one know this. Also, this was in the seventies. No one leave China then. So live in another country very hard do. And then he say very strange thing. He say I will have Western student—how you say?— apprentice."

"Did he say the name Peter?"Dr. Chow shakes his head. "Did not say. And he say I also teach young boy with great ability."

"Did you ever visit this psychic again?"

"Did one time. But he die already."

I speculate aloud about the episode of *Ripley's Believe It or Not* that featured Dr. Chow. What if I had not watched it? Dr. Chow says it would not have mattered because our meeting was *yuen fun*, and then he translates: "already written." At one point, he says, he was going to locate the new clinic three houses down from mine. Somehow, he says, our paths would have crossed.

Not fate, but a dedication borne of fascination brings me to the clinic day after day, week after week for the next several months. One evening I pause at the office door and ask Dr. Chow about the lump-sum payment. Without raising his eyes from his paper work, he says there are more important things to consider than money. Slowly he lifts his head and fixes me with his gaze. In a quiet measured tone, he says I must start to prepare for the big test.

"Big test? What big test?" His mouth turns up at the corners, and a glint of merriment brightens his eyes. For a moment his face takes on the supple contours of youth. He tries to conceal his enjoyment, but the effort is in vain. "What big test?" I repeat.

"Must find out yourself what big test is. Finding out is part of big test." The words hang in the air like a message written in smoke.

"How can I prepare for the big test if I don't know what the big test is?" He replies that if I keep practicing my chi kung, the requirements of the big test will one day reveal themselves to me. He adds that this will not happen for some time.

"In what way will I learn about the requirements of the big test?" I ask. "Surely you can tell me that." The doctor will not be duped into providing any more information. Instead he crosses his arms and shakes his head, shaking the smile from his face. "But what if I don't pass the big test? What happens then?"

"Apprenticeship ends. You leave clinic." He picks up his pen and bends his head to his papers. He does not look up again, and so I turn and take myself out of the room, my heart pounding crazily.

*Pythagoras said that the most divine art was
that of healing. And if the healing art is most divine
it must occupy itself with the soul as well as the body.*

—Appollonius of Tyana

Standing Chi Kung

I am impatient to make progress with my practice. I want
to be prepared for the big test whenever it comes, in whatever form it might take. To strengthen my chi I try to
manipulate it with my mind, sending it by thought-power (the
Chinese say "mind-will") to different parts of my body. As I
describe my experiments to Fanny, the new receptionist, Alan's
fluting voice interrupts from the hallway.

"Don't control chi," he says, his arms full of clean white
sheets for the examining tables. "This wrong attitude for now.
This make your chi practice into activity. It's not activity. It's
enjoyment, it's learning. Just follow chi with your mind."

In a synchronistic moment worthy of Carl Jung, I go home
and pluck a random book from my bookshelf—it is the *Tao Te
Ching*—and therein I read: "To control chi with the mind is to be
aggressive. Things decay when they are too aggressive. This is not
the Tao. This ends soon."

But what is the Tao? The Tao, when it has been translated, is frequently referred to as "the way of nature," "the way of the universe," or simply "the way." The Jesuit missionaries in China considered the Tao to be Logos or God. Perhaps Jung's definition of the Tao—bringing what is unconscious to what is conscious—is also helpful if we consider that following the Tao may include understanding the nature and existence of chi.

It is a red-letter day when Dr. Chow promotes me to the standing position. But ten minutes into the standing position I realize what a sweet life I had when still a sitter. Now I have to stand in one place for half an hour or more, with my feet shoulder-width apart, my knees slightly bent, and my palms held two feet away from my belly as if holding a large beach ball. The position tires me, though the sensation of chi in my limbs is noticeably stronger. Because the chi from my body is supercharging the room, Dr. Chow instructs me to sweep the air with my hands at the end of each session and massage the collected energy into my dan tian. This is not packing or storing energy such as martial artists describe when they talk about building up the body for fighting—for that is the practice of hard chi kung. What I am doing is simply corralling errant chi and bringing it back home.

In the middle of my third standing session, I am feeling drowsily at peace with the world, and I roll onto the bed for a rest. Hardly have I shut my eyes when the door swings open, revealing Dr. Chow in a rectangle of light. "You lazy!" he cries. "You never pass big test this way!" In fright I jump off the examining table, and as he shuts the door I resume the standing position, my pulse bumping against my wrist.

Many times I wonder whether I have the single-minded focus required of a serious student. At home I do not practice every night and every morning as I have pledged to do—there are too many distractions. If Aristotle was correct when he said that our unique excellence is also our tragic flaw, then my unique excellence is my interest in a wide variety of things, one of which is chi kung. And my tragic flaw is my interest in a wide variety of things, all of which take me away from my chi kung.

After six weeks of standing chi kung the position has become bearable, but not pleasurable. The effects of the chi itself, though, are invigorating. As I describe to Dr. Chow the new pathways forged by the chi, he comments that my chi is tracing out the meridian lines of different organs, strengthening them and improving their efficiency. This will prolong my life, he says, and prevent premature aging. I ask him if it is true that he is over three hundred years old, and he says yes, give or take two hundred and fifty years.

History does not record how the knowledge of meridian lines came about, but I think it is reasonable to suppose that early chi kung practitioners discovered the lines of energy through internal observation, a discovery confirmed by other practitioners and later codified through experiments with acupuncture. Artist-shamans from antiquity have depicted similar lines of energy in their x-ray paintings of humans and animals, paintings found in caves around the world.

Perhaps the early practitioners of chi kung, who number among our first scientists, also discovered that too much sex weakens the energy field. This discovery, in turn, might have formed the basis of certain celibacy practices whose practical origins later became obscured in the moral strictures of organized religion. My enforced celibacy has thankfully ended, but if I have once again entered the world of earthly delights, I am not the voluptuary I might have been. Nature has decreed that one cannot be both a great lover and a great healer at the same time. And if you are but a lowly chi kung practitioner who is trying to raise his level of chi, you will be the Least, rather than the Last, of the Red Hot Lovers. In chi kung, love of wisdom replaces love of pleasure, or so the theory goes. This was also the way of Aristotle. For Aristotle, to love wisdom was to undergo an act of conversion.

To be a philosopher was to change one's life, not just one's thinking.

Recently Dr. Chow has given me permission to read books on chi kung, and after one of the standing sessions, I take a seat in his office and tell him most of the books recommend keeping the tongue pressed against the roof of the palate when practicing. Without the tongue in this position, say the authors, the body's electrical circuit will be broken.

Dr. Chow shifts his chair closer to me in friendship and collegiality and says that he does not teach this method to his students, not because it is wrong, but because his chi is potent enough to jump over any break in the circuit. Peter's own experience, he says, confirms this. I tell him that some of the books suggest tapping your kidneys to stimulate kidney chi. Dr. Chow's response is swift and immediate.

"I don't teach this method. Might damage kidneys."

"I've also read about Taoist methods of cultivating chi through various sexual practices."

"This method also have danger. Can lose chi this way. Even lose little bit, not good. My students have success without this method, so no need." I have always been curious about the factors involved in the selection of his students. When I ask him for an explanation, he swallows before answering, and I remember reading somewhere that saliva is replete with chi. He then parts his lips and speaks again. "If patient can benefit from chi kung training, then I teach."

"So you teach everyone?"

"Not this way."

"What way is it then?"

"Sometime patient not good character. And I no teach."

"How can you tell if a patient doesn't have a good character?"

Dr. Chow throws himself back in his chair as if pondering how much to reveal. He draws a breath and says, "I throw chi at head and look at aura. If aura turns black, I no teach." Never before have I heard him speak about the concept of an aura. I marvel that he even knows the English word.

"But if a student has a good character, you'll teach?" I ask.

"Even good student not ready sometime. You not ready when I meet you first time. Then you got ready."

Why I was not ready the first time, I have no idea. Maybe I was deficient in some essential quality. I ask him what qualities a student should have, and he tells me that a student should have intelligence, dedication, discipline, patience, a good character, and a good heart. Then he says a good student is only half the equation, for a good student needs a good teacher. And a good teacher must possess the same qualities as the student, but also have something worthwhile to teach. He smiles at me with his aura-opened eyes, and I return the smile, aura-blind. But the subject of auras I will not let pass unremarked.

"If you can see someone's aura," I say, "can you diagnose someone's illness just by looking at their energy blueprint?"

"Don't do diagnosis this way. Use traditional method."

"Is it because psychic diagnosis isn't scientific?" I ask, knowing his high regard for the scientific method. He replies that psychic diagnosis could be considered scientific if it was tested and found accurate. And there are certain advantages to psychic diagnosis, he says, because it can operate as a kind of x-ray. A doctor can detect kidney stones this way, for example, without exposing the patient to the harmful effects of x-rays. "Then why don't you do it?" I ask.

"First, Western patient not so comfortable with this method because no proof. Second, this psychic diagnosis take energy. In my clinic have seven rooms for patients, and sometimes rooms filled all day. If use aura technique, then have less energy give patient."

By degrees the standing chi kung position begins to build endurance in my body. Then, just as I become accustomed to the position, Dr. Chow comes into the room and changes it. No longer will I hold my hands in front of my abdomen, he explains. Instead I will hold my hands at the level of my head, a foot away, palms facing each other. Upon adopting the new position, I discover my arms tire quickly, and from time to time I drop them back to my sides.

Weeks pass. One day Dr. Chow comes into my room and changes my position yet again. In the new position my hands are held three feet from my forehead and turned slightly toward each other. This position, Dr. Chow tells me, is simple but powerful and has been passed down for generations in his family. In all the books I have read on chi kung, I have yet to see this simple position described or illustrated.

Dr. Chow explains that with the right palm facing the left— yin and yang—an energy field forms around the head that nourishes the brain, eyes, and face. He adds that many positions described in books, both ancient and modern, do not take into account the body's polarities. Of course, any exercise will produce a certain amount of chi, but this does not mean a strong field of energy is always produced. He concludes by saying, "Most chi kung position you find in book, only good for exercise."

With the new standing position I repeatedly experience what seems to be an optical illusion—lines of energy stream from the fingers of both hands and join in mid-space. Many times my fingers feel as if they will burst open at the tips, like the ladyfinger firecrackers I exploded when I was a boy. After a few weeks of rehearsing this position, the chi suddenly grows stronger, and now it thrums in my body like a great vibrating gourd. In kind and quality it is unlike anything I have ever felt. To the outside world my accomplishment—the chi's accomplishment—is of no great consequence. But I am standing atop John Muir's mountaintop, and from my mouth come his words, "Here all the world's prizes seem as nothing."

Remain relaxed and in the
vastness and the chi will follow.

—The Yellow Emperor's Classic of Internal Medicine

A Stationary Feast

Dr. Chow is an ethical omnivore. Eating chicken builds up energy faster than a diet of strictly vegetables, he tells me, as we take a table in a Chinese restaurant. He continues on the theme, saying he could not dispense the amount of chi he does on a daily basis without eating meat on occasion. We are waiting for my friend Tamiyo to arrive before we order, and I tell him I maintain a meatless diet for my own reasons. He nods with understanding and says some masters can survive without eating any food at all. They live, he says, on the minute amounts of chi they ingest from the air and from the liquids they drink. He adds that archeologists discovered in the Han tomb at Mawangdui, Chang Sha, Hunan Province, a book written on silk over two thousand years ago, called *On Abandoning Food and Living on Chi*. But masters who live on air and liquids, he adds, cannot throw chi very often or they would quickly deplete their store of energy.

The waitress materializes and upturns our cups and places a pot of tea at the center of the table. Dr. Chow pours the green tea to the rims just as a smiling woman approaches the table. Tamiyo is sweet-scented and beautiful, and as she pulls back a chair, she attracts glances from around the room. I met Tamiyo a month earlier while we were fluttering our arms in the Tai Chi class taught by Dr. Chow in the basement of his clinic. Heart fluttering soon followed, and Tamiyo and I are now dating. Dr. Chow turns to the waitress, forgoes ordering his regular dishes out of consideration for me—not necessary, I tell him —and instead orders steamed and sauteed vegetables of every variety with plates of braised and fried tofu.

Egg-drop soup begins the meal. As he ladles out the soup into three small bowls, he tells us egg yolks are good for the brain. The main dishes are served, and the din of conversation rises in the room. As I sample my first mouthful of tofu, Dr. Chow leans over and whispers in my ear, "Too much tofu lessen your sex drive." The warning takes me by surprise, but he is talking to me outside the boundaries of the apprenticeship, as one regular guy to another.

We dine in great content. One of the vegetable dishes has a strong flavoring of garlic, and the doctor tells us garlic improves every organ except the eyes, on which it has no effect. Tamiyo is wearing a silver necklace with colored stones, and Dr. Chow remarks upon its beauty. I take this opportunity to ask him about another kind of stone, also of great beauty, a stone that is said to be found in the ashes of cremated yogis. Stones such as these are alleged to contain great power, I tell him, and I ask if such stones are ever found in the cremated remains of chi kung masters. On Dr. Chow's face there is a look of faint surprise. *Where does Peter hear of such things?* He wipes his mouth with his napkin and then speaks.

"This also can happen with ashes of chi kung master," he says. "Can find stones red, yellow, green, blue, purple, and crystal-colored. We call them *saylehtze*."

"Where do they come from in the body, these stones?" I ask. He corrects the position of my fingers on my chopsticks and watches intently as I pick up a slippery snow pea. Satisfied with my effort, he returns to the question.

"No one know where stone come from. And no one know exactly how stone is made. But chi kung master create these stone in the body and later can draw chi from them." I tell him that in other healing traditions, when they find these stones in the ashes, they use them for healing. He holds his head to one side, considering. "In China, not this way. Only for reverence." Tamiyo, who is wielding her chopsticks perfectly, says similar stones are supposedly found in the ashes of certain Buddhist monks from Tibet, and these stones are referred to as "Tibetan drops."

"Isn't it?" Dr. Chow says and pops a piece of steamed broccoli in his mouth.

Tamiyo talks about the differences between Mahayana Buddhism and Theraveda Buddhism, the two great systems that purport to represent the Buddha's teachings. One of the differences between the two schools, she says, is that Mahayana Buddhists believe that psychic powers can be of help to others. Theraveda Buddhists, on the other hand, believe these powers can hinder a person's enlightenment.

Dr. Chow raps his forefinger on the table. "Both right." The waitress sets a fresh pot of tea on the table, and Tamiyo asks Dr. Chow if he ever experimented with the powers he received from his chi kung practice. He pours out the tea. "When I was younger, did experiment, but now save all my chi for patient and student."

"But don't you want to know what you can do?"

"I know what I can do," he says in a subdued voice.

The conversation shifts to the mundane, and he talks about how he wants to remodel the basement in the clinic for his Tai Chi class. As he speaks, I can sense a lightness seep into the ming men point in my lower back, a lightness that quickly transforms into a circling ball of fire, with heat diffusing into my kidneys, and then the chi elongates up my spine in an arrow of hot shooting light. I look over at Dr. Chow. He is still talking to Tamiyo and has given no indication that he has done anything unusual. I let my body relax, and the chi grows stronger. Tamiyo asks Dr. Chow how much a person should practice if they want to develop extraordinary health and powers, and Dr. Chow says as much as possible.

"What's the maximum practice time?" she asks.

"No maximum," comes the answer.

She looks at him with dazzled eyes. "But a person has to sleep," she says.

He shoots her an amused look. "Some chi kung master no have bed. Instead, they—"

"No bed?" I interrupt.

"They meditate all night," he says.

"But they must sleep sometime," Tamiyo says.

Dr. Chow shakes his head. "If sleep, they no meditate, so they no sleep."

"Not ever?" she asks. He shakes his head again.

"Surely they must dream," I say.

"If dream, then this sleep," he corrects.

"Do you think that practicing chi kung is better than sleeping?" I ask.

"If ask this question, then don't understand chi kung." He goes on to explain that after practicing chi kung all night, the body is entirely refreshed in the morning because chi has circulated many times through the meridians. I counter that there must be advantages to sleep that chi kung cannot provide. He furrows his brow in thought and then nods, saying that sometimes in your sleep you can receive an answer to a question. And sometimes you just want to sleep, he adds. With his devotion to the concrete facts of experience, he suggests I practice chi kung for the entire night and see the results for myself. I ask if it is necessary to have this level of endurance for the big test. He replies that what is necessary is that I practice as much as I can.

The check comes, and Dr. Chow drains his tea and snaps his credit card onto the tray. I thank him for the meal, and he focuses his eyes an inch above my head and says that I will have a gold credit card within three months. The prediction takes me by surprise. I have not even applied for a gold card, and I have been in the working world only a short while. As we get up from the table, I quietly allude to the chi he has slipped me, and he smiles, saying nothing.

At eleven o'clock that night I begin practicing standing chi kung in my bedroom, and by a rending effort of the will I make it into the wee hours of the morning until fatigue finally crashes over me, the whole room heaving like the sea. I cannot recall the exact time I tumble into bed, but I do know that when I pull up the covers, there is chi running exultantly through the twelve meridians and the eight extraordinary channels. And while I sleep, the chi still flows. Even in my dreams it is flowing, and when I awake in the morning it is there again, electric, exhilarating, exciting.

In the morning, walking through a stand of pine trees in the park, I am struck by the vivid green boughs, the sharp scent of the pine needles, the tang of the air on my tongue, the cracking sound of the forest floor under my feet. This is life as it is meant to be, I think to myself. This is experiencing the world in real truth.

In the mail, two months later, I receive a gold card from the bank.

When Healers Become Patients

Reiki master, shiatsu practitioner, chiropractor, massage therapist—the profession matters not. Into the clinic these healers all drag their worn bodies, looking slightly chagrined, as if their new status as patients casts doubt on their healing abilities.

One day a Reiki master walks into the clinic, looking haggard and spent. But the young female apprentice who accompanies him is full of vitality. The two of them speak to Dr. Chow privately, receive their treatments, and leave. Afterward, I venture inside the office and ask Dr. Chow about their medical conditions. He tells me the apprentice has been stealing the master's energy—unbeknownst to both the master and the apprentice. He did not tell them what was occuring, he says, because he did not wish to break the bond of the apprenticeship. Students often take their teacher's energy without knowing it, he explains. Now it is my turn to look chagrined. How many times have I sat in his office and taken his energy without knowing it? How else to explain my constant rejuvenation in his presence?

I ask if there is any way a healer can prevent giving away his personal energy to a patient. Dr. Chow screws his features into a frown. As a doctor, he says, he can say with certainty that healers lose a bit of energy every time they heal. I tell him some healers claim the energy they give is from the earth, or from the universe, or that it is the energy of love. Dr. Chow replies that where the energy originates from is of no consequence—it passes through the healer's body, so it will always take some of the healer's personal energy. The trick, he says, is knowing how to regenerate one's energy in such quantities that passing it to others does not adversely affect one's health. As an afterthought he adds that people are always taking and giving energy to one another. And he cites the example of group meditation, where people with high amounts of energy lose some to those with low amounts of energy. It is a matter of physics, he says.

A Chinese healer enters the clinic, and he is struggling, struggling even for a gulp of air. By his own account, he is an advanced chi kung practitioner, but he barely has enough energy to cross the floor of the waiting room. Once he leaves the premises, I ask Dr. Chow about him, and the doctor, sitting in his office, folds his arms.

"This patient practice chi kung wrong way. Learn from master in Hong Kong."

"How did the patient practice?"

"He force breath down."

"Can you fix him?"

"This take long time. Maybe not can fix. Chi kung practice should be natural, breath easy, no force."

From reading the *Tao Te Ching*, I know that in the old days men used to breathe all the way down to their heels. I repeat this Taoist aphorism to Dr. Chow and say if people practiced like this in the old days, then why not in modern times? Dr. Chow hesitates a moment. "Can do this way. But must have good kung fu. Not for most people today, not for this patient. Too dangerous. If Peter recommend this way, people get very sick. Peter want get sued?" His merry eyes indicate this is in the nature of a joke, and I laugh.

I ask Dr. Chow what other healers he has helped. He says he recently met with a healer who had a gouty foot, but he did not treat her. I am astounded and ask him why. He tells me the healer, a woman, is a chi kung master, or at least claims to be. During the consultation, the woman told him that no chi kung master can throw chi more than a few inches and that anyone who claims otherwise is a charlatan. I ask what he said to her in return. He says he told her everyone needs to be aware of charlatans in the healing field. But he disagreed that chi can only be thrown a few inches and told her to review some of the research in China. He also told her that since she was a chi kung master she should heal her foot herself but that if her foot was still troubling her in a few weeks, then he would gladly treat it. The woman left the clinic, he says, and has not returned.

"So perhaps she is a chi kung master, after all," I say.

"She have lots of knowledge," he says, "but no power."

"How do you know she has no power?"

"Can tell how much chi a person has just by looking."

A saffron-robed monk of an advanced age holds open the door for several seconds before stepping inside. His eyes, framed by gold-rimmed spectacles, give the clinic a swift appraisal, and to no one in particular he delivers his opinion, in an orotund voice, that the energy here is good and that if it were not to his liking he would leave immediately. Upon the couch he lowers his great heft, the breadth of his upper chest lapsing into a genial rotundity around his waist. He stares briefly at me in the chair opposite and then turns his shaved, globular head toward the office window. A sigh escapes his mouth. The doctor is conferring with a patient.

Moved by some reflex of respect, I ask the old monk if he would like some water. A raspy noise comes from his throat as he repeats the word *water*, so I bring him a cup and ask where he is from. He hollows one hand around his ear, and I ask the question again. "Korea," he says in a deep ringing voice. "I had a hospital there, over two hundred beds, but I gave away all of my chi energy, and so I had to leave."

"And so you're here to see the doctor about—"

"No reason," he interrupts. " Just to see him." I take a seat on one of the chairs. Here, evidently, is a doctor of high honor who likes to confer with other doctors of high honor. "Who are you?" he asks suddenly in a masterful tone, looking me full in the face. I give him my name, and he raises his hand to his ear. I give my name once more.

"I'm not interested in the name on your driver's license. Who are you?"

"A writer," I say loudly.

"I'm not interested in your profession. Who are you?"

He has the bantering rhythm of a Zen master, and I decide to play along. "I'm a man."

Out shoots a hand to correct me. "If you define yourself by your gender you can never see anything clearly. Now, who are you?"

"A human being," I say. He cups his ear. "A human being!" I shout.

A flicker of surprise widens his eyes. "Very good. If you're a human being, you're part of the great sea of humanity—as are we all." To this I assent with a nod. He asks for a paper and pen, and I fetch them. "I will give you a gift today," he says in a low vibrating voice, and he draws on the paper a large circumflex to represent a mountain. At the base of the mountain he makes a mark. "In terms of energy, this is humanity," he says. A little further up the mountain he makes another mark. "This is the level you have attained." I want to ask how he knows this, but something in his eyes compels me to silence, and, besides, I do not feel like shouting any more. Further up the mountain he makes another mark. "This is the height your teacher will help you reach. Any higher you reach by yourself." I wonder if he is referring to the big test in any way, but already he is making another mark higher up the mountain. "This is where I am. And this is also where your teacher is. We both need to climb a few steps higher and jump off the precipice into the void."

He puts the pen aside and grumbles for more water. I bring him another cup, and he drinks it down in a gulp. Without a word of warning he then proceeds to tell me of some major events that will occur in my future—some pleasant, some unpleasant. Listening to the unpleasant predictions, I tell myself they are only warnings to be heeded. The pleasant predictions, I tell myself, will undoubtedly come to pass.

The patient in the office now sallies forth into the waiting room, and the monk gets to his feet and shuffles off to see the doctor but not before giving me a nod, like a priest bestowing a benediction. For the next several minutes the monk and the doctor speak in long undertones out of all possible earshot, and I realize that what is passing between them will remain a secret. At the end of the discussion, the monk pushes open the office door from his chair and beckons me. I come forward quickly and stand in the doorway. Regarding me sideways he says he has something to tell me, and then he shoots an unexpected bolt. "Your teacher is lonely for a wife."

I am taken aback and have no response. Dr. Chow looks up at me, and his eyes seek some kind of understanding. I try to communicate—with my thoughts, my feelings—that I understand. I know he wants a family, and I also know that one day he will have what he wants. But what is the point of the monk revealing Dr. Chow's emotional state to me?

After the monk leaves, Dr. Chow asks in a quiet voice for my thoughts, and I tell him I have none. For a moment the doctor looks pensive and then says: "This monk interesting." I mention the monk's predictions about my life, searching the doctor's steady eyes for a reaction. With a nod of his head, the doctor confirms everything. Then he digs me gently in the ribs and smiles. "And your children will be spoiled." Children? I am not even married. I wait to hear no more and flee the clinic without a word of apology or regret.

Moving Chi Kung

Emerging from the clinic room, I hear an unfamiliar voice in the hallway. A soft-featured woman is speaking in Chinese to Dr. Chow. Hearing my footsteps, the doctor turns to me. "Peter like to see moving chi kung?"

"Yes, Peter would."

Dr. Chow speaks quietly to the woman, and she closes her eyes. Almost immediately her body begins to tremble. As the doctor massages the air in her direction, the chi causes her trembling body to uproot itself, and she begins to stagger around the hallway like a drunk. I glance at her face. Her features are suffused with a serenity that belies her shaking body. About to strike herself against the sharp edge of a counter, she is saved at the last second by Dr. Chow who catches her and spins her in a new direction. Without interruption she continues her short staccato steps with a touch of froth at her lips until the doctor notches up the tempo with a twist of his hand, and her feet stomp the floor like a flamenco dancer gone berserk. Shake, shake, shake until her frail body nearly shakes itself asunder. Dr. Chow halts the demonstration suddenly by gripping the arm of the woman and speaking something low in her ear. The woman takes a deep shuddering breath and then smiles at me through shy, peeping eyes.

"This why no like to practice chi kung by myself," she says.

Is this my future as a chi kung student? I am beginning to doubt my resolve to train for the big test. The next day I ask Dr. Chow if my training will lead to such uncontrolled movements. He explains that shaking occurs in the body when chi affects the nerves. But my body, he says, is not so sensitive. I nod my head, not sure whether I have just received a compliment or an insult. I ask Dr. Chow who the strange woman was. His face lights with pride. "Oh, this my sister."

I am listening to the sound of a galloping horse, but I am not in the countryside. I am inside a clinic room with the door shut. After my session I report the sound to Dr. Chow, and he says the owner of the long, galloping legs is Joanne Brackeen, the noted jazz pianist and composer. He says the chi affects the nerves in Joanne's body in such a way that she is compelled to run on the spot. One day I meet Joanne in the waiting room, and she invites me into a clinic room where I watch her pound the floor like a Masai dancer. Joanne is not exhausted by her exertions, but instead looks refreshed and even exhilarated.

The presence of chi in her body has another consequence that I hear one evening while deep in the throes of my practice. Joanne begins to burp. No—burping does not do justice to the deep guttural stretches of sound that come echoing from her belly. Joanne is belching, and the belches follow one upon the other in a kind of gastric metronome, resounding through the clinic. There and then I swear a dark oath that if ever I begin to belch I will quit my chi kung practice once and for all—big test be damned.

Later, when I ask Dr. Chow about Joanne's belching, he explains that bodily noises are not uncommon during intense chi kung practice. "Chi know what it must do to make someone healthy," he says. Joanne thinks of her side effects as amusing. Often times, she says, just thinking about the belching chi makes her laugh.

O, chi of many faces: mystic, healer, sage—and now, court jester.

Let your medicine be your food
and your food be your medicine.

—Hippocrates

The Herb of Deathlessness

I have a photograph of an ancient Chinese painting that depicts a traditional Chinese doctor standing beside a deer. In one hand, the doctor holds a gourd and in the other, a basket of peaches and a bouquet of oddly-shaped flowers. I give the photograph to Dr. Chow who studies it at his desk, and he glances up from the photograph and says the gourd is a hollowed-out plant that was once used to transport medicine. Deer horn, he says, was known to strengthen the kidneys. And at one time, he adds, peaches were believed to promote longevity.

With a finger I trace the bouquet. "And these flowers?"

"Oh, this not flower. This *ling zhi.*"

"Ling zhi?"

"Special mushroom."

"Special in what way?" I ask.

The Chinese character *ling*, he explains, contains the pictures of a shaman, falling rain, and the act of making a prayer, so it means spiritual power. The character *zhi* refers to the fungus of trees and elixirs of longevity. So together the two words mean the herb of deathlessness. I ask what the herb can be used for, and he lifts his arms, ebullient. "For everything!"

"Then why is it not prescribed all the time?"

"Western scientist need experiment more. Also, most time the ling zhi you will find has only little power. Good ling zhi hard to find." He leans back in his chair, throws his right leg over his left, and with a faraway look begins recounting a story. It is the story of the ling zhi's origins, and it takes place in the time of Shih Huang Ti, China's First Emperor, the so-called Yellow Emperor, who is remembered today for the Great Wall.

The Emperor, Dr. Chow says, had heard from his ministers that a certain mushroom could bring the dead back to life. The mushroom was known as a chi plant, because it distributed chi throughout the body. Villagers in the mountains had observed seabirds with a strange plant in their beaks and concluded that the plant must grow on an island.

Telling the story, Dr. Chow fills the small room with his radiance, and I can feel my whole body vibrating at a higher level. He goes on to say that the Emperor charged his top officer, Admiral Hsu Fu, with a mission to find the chi plant. The Admiral set sail with hundreds of subjects, but was never seen again. According to legend, the Admiral discovered the land of Wa—Japan—and colonized it.

"I hope you return from Los Angeles," the doctor says to me with a smile, referring to the vacation I am to take the next day.

"Maybe I won't come back," I say, "and instead I'll start my own little colony." With the greatest economy of movement he rises from his chair, comes around the desk, and rests a gentle hand on my shoulder.

"Peter like these palm trees more than he know," he says in a cryptic whisper.

On my trip to Los Angeles I make an excursion to Chinatown where I find some ling zhi, and it is not inexpensive. The Asian herbalist, who has trained in Shanghai, tells me it is *ganoderma oregonense*, a species grown in Oregon. When I ask him about the efficacy of the healing fungus, he tells me the Japanese government has approved it as a substance to treat cancer.

"You understand chi?" he asks.

"A little."

"The ling zhi builds up every kind of chi in the body, especially *wei* chi, which is the chi that protects the body from disease. The ling zhi can destroy any intruder."

I bring the Oregon ling zhi back to Toronto and present it with great flourish to Dr. Chow in his office. "How about a little herb of deathlessness?" I say, unwrapping my treasure. Dr. Chow brightens, and then runs a hand over his jaw.

"This ling zhi," he says, "not have much power."

"How can you tell?" Abruptly he stands up, excuses himself for a moment, and leaves the office. I never mind waiting in his office—in fact, I relish any time spent there. The office is a veritable sea of chi, and I can feel my body floating in it, suspended in it. Footsteps on the ceiling above my head—Dr. Chow is upstairs in his apartment. I am suddenly seized with the desire to climb the narrow staircase that leads upstairs, just to see how this man lives, but the thought disappears a moment later when Dr. Chow returns with a mysterious object in his hands. Big as a bowling ball, the object is swathed in layers of plastic wrapping. Layer by layer, he removes the wrapping, and my eyes open wide at the contents. It is a giant mushroom, unlike anything else I have ever seen.

"Ling zhi," says Dr. Chow matter-of-factly. The mushroom is thick and black, with the dark color saturating its entire shape. But there is something even more startling about the mushroom. It has a shimmering radiance.

"There's a light coming from the ling zhi!" I say.

Dr. Chow nods sagely. "This ling zhi have power."

I ask how it came into his possession, and a wistful expression plays across his face. "Before I leave China, master give to me", he says.His master had no money, he adds, and this was the most valuable thing the master could give. Of course, he says, this gift is worth more than any amount of money. I ask about the mushroom's reputed healing abilities. Can it really bring someone back from the dead? Almost, he says. I ask if the master put his chi into the ling zhi or if the radiance comes from the ling zhi itself. The ling zhi has its own power, he explains, but the master also gave it chi.

"Who was this master, Dr. Chow? What was his name?"

"Lee Chun-choy," says Dr. Chow, and his eyes grow misty.

I am curious to know where the master obtained the mushroom, but it is an answer Dr. Chow cannot provide, because the master never told him. I know from my reading that an herb as wild and rare as this one must have been gathered from a remote mountain area. The Chinese have always valued herbs that grow in inaccessible places, because the hardier the herb, the higher its level of chi.

Dr. Chow begins wrapping up the ling zhi in its plastic wrapper and then pauses for a moment. "This good you can see chi. Must be able to see chi if want to become a chi kung master. In old days everyone see chi rising from chi kung master, like steam. Later generation, they no can see chi. Later generation not so sensitive." He shakes his head at the state of humanity and then leaves the office with his consecrated cargo balanced in his hands like an enormous jewel.

The Prodigy

Technically, Joseph and I are at the same level—we are both practicing standing chi kung—but years of practicing meditation and martial arts have heightened his sensitivity to an extraordinary degree. He has come from Los Angeles to study with Dr. Chow for the summer and works part-time as the clinic receptionist. In his early twenties, he still looks sixteen, and his slight frame does nothing to dispel the illusion.

I am watching Dr. Chow as he plants his feet at the end of the hallway and caresses the air with his hands as if he were conducting an invisible orchestra. Joseph, his eyes shut, positioned at the other end of the hallway, reports in a loud voice where the chi is striking his body. Each correct answer occasions another throw of chi until Dr. Chow drops his hands to his side and in a booming voice congratulates Joseph on his accomplishment.

Joseph is a solitary person and, from what I can tell, perfectly suited to the life of a chi kung master. Not until two weeks before his departure for Los Angeles am I able to spend time with him, so intent is he on his practice. At a coffee shop late one afternoon, I ask Joseph if he has taken the big test yet. He says he has not, but he knows that catching chi from a distance is part of the test. I ask how he knows this, and he says one day he felt a strong sensation of chi while passing by Dr. Chow's clinic. He looked around. Dr. Chow was standing across the street, waving at him with a mischievous grin. Later on, in the clinic, Dr. Chow told him that to pass the big test, a person must be able to catch chi from a distance. Joseph's eyes fasten on mine, and in a voice tinged with regret he tells me that he will never know what the big test is because he is going to law school in the fall.

"Law school? But you're so talented in chi kung."

He takes a sip of his Diet Coke and laughs softly. "Not when you consider what the real masters are capable of. And temperamentally I'm unsuited to the lifestyle. I'm too Western in my thinking." He pauses as a pretty woman walks past our table. "There are two women I'm interested in right now," he says, turning back to me, "but my hands are tied because I'm practicing intensive chi kung. I have to do that celibacy thing." He rolls his eyes and laughs at his predicament.

"Will you still practice chi kung when you move back to Los Angeles?" He assures me he will. As if to adduce evidence of his dedication, he says wherever he goes, he always draws energy from flowers, plants, trees, animals. I listen with envy and ask how he does it. He brings his chair closer to the table. "Oh, the technique is simple. I hold my hands over whatever energy source I want to tap into and imagine the energy flowing into the lao gong point of my palms."

"What do you do with the energy once you get it?"

"Sometimes I store the energy like this—" He rubs his left palm in a circle on his abdomen. "And sometimes I circulate the energy around my body." I ask him from what other sources he draws his energy. "Oh, mostly I get it through meditation," he says. "But when I was younger, sometimes I took it from strangers." He smiles at my startled expression. "I know, it was a

really stupid thing to do," he says. "And I didn't take a lot of energy, just a little, but I got sick one day and realized I had caught an
illness from one of the strangers. Instant karma!" he says with a
contrite smile. "Oh, damn!" he says suddenly. "I'm going to get
soaked!"

Rain is lashing against the windows of the coffee shop, and
Joseph has to meet a relative downtown. As we pay the bill, I tell
him I feel chi more strongly when it rains outside. I tell him I
practice in the bathroom sometimes with the shower running,
and this boosts my chi as well. Joseph's eyebrows lift in arcs of
astonishment, and he says he will try the technique himself.

When I arrive at the clinic the next morning, I find Joseph
sitting behind the reception window, his eyes alight with excitement. "So last night I ran the shower," he says, "and a heavy mist
filled the bathroom. I was taking my shirt off to begin practicing
when my upper back began rippling with chi. I mean, it was so
strong I actually looked over my shoulder in the mirror to see if I
could detect any bumps on the surface of my skin." I give him a
look of surprise. "No, there weren't any ripples on my skin, but
that's how intense it felt. And then I got this idea that maybe I
could practice in the shower itself, and so I tried it, but it didn't
work."

Dr. Chow comes out of his office, greets us both, and tells me
to go inside and practice. Before I leave for my room, Joseph says
he will show me his favorite meditation spot at the end of the
day. A few hours later we stamp off into the sunshine, heading for
a nearby park. Along the way Joseph shows me how he procures
energy from a row of bushes by trailing his hand a few inches
above the foliage and then rubbing his abdomen afterward. Next,
he stoops to examine a flower and cups his hands around the
petals without touching them and then rubs his face with the
collected chi. When we reach the park, he leads me to an enormous willow tree whose trunk measures some twenty feet in cir-
cumference. With knees slightly bent, he shuts his eyes and

stretches out his arms as if to embrace the tree but does not touch it.

As he is performing this maneuver, a plump woman packaged into a business suit stops to observe, her dachshund pausing beside her. I inform Joseph that we are under surveillance, but he maintains his motionless stance even when the dog begins barking. From his beatific expression I can tell he is in another world. His eyes open suddenly, and he asks if I would like to try. The plump woman has not budged an inch, and I shoot her a weak smile before I step forward and imitate Joseph's stance in front of the tree. For a moment there is no sensation, but Joseph tells me to persevere, and minutes later I feel a strange sensation along my arms—an army of marching ants.

I pull away and open my eyes, but there are no marching ants. It is only the marching chi, and I close my eyes and extend my arms once again. The tree's energy has a rough, spiky texture, and as it mingles with my own energy the resultant mixture moves thickly through my limbs. After ten minutes I step back from the tree, inarticulate with amazement.

"Now try the other side of the tree," Joseph suggests. The other side of the tree is in the shadows, and when I step over the massive roots, I notice the plump woman is walking her dog now, our little novelty act filed away in her brain, no doubt, as an amusing story for the dinner table. As I resume my stance, the tree's energy drips into my arms like slow sap. When I describe my sensations to Joseph, he nods in agreement. "On the sunny side, the energy is stronger," he says.

He tells me he comes to the park almost every day. He says Dr. Chow knows about his technique of drawing chi from nature, but has not commented on it except to say that many people practice this technique in China. Joseph tells me he learned this technique from some ancient illustrated manuscripts that his parents brought back from Shanghai. Most of the manuscripts, he says, advocated the use of pine trees when practicing chi kung outdoors—the needles themselves are conductors of chi—but one manuscript had recommended using a willow tree.

The next evening Joseph comes over to my house to conduct some more experiments. After charging ourselves up in separate rooms, we meet in the living room and stand with our palms facing each other, about six inches apart. Slowly I move my hands, first to the left, then to the right. Like the famous episode of *I Love Lucy*, in which Lucy mirrors every movement of Harpo Marx, Joseph moves his hands in a mirror image of my own—but unlike Harpo, Joseph has his eyes shut. We switch roles. This time I must follow Joseph's lead, but I do not have his level of sensitivity and can only match his basic moves. I am deflated. At this rate I will never pass the big test.

A day before his return to Los Angeles, Joseph phones me and says in an anxious voice that we have to get together immediately. Something extraordinary has happened, he says. We meet at the entrance to the park, and as we walk inside, he can barely contain his excitement. "I was on the bus, staring at this woman, and suddenly I saw her past life! And then I saw another past life! Every five seconds—a new past life!" It is entirely new to his experience, he says, and he has no idea what to make of it.

I ask if he will demonstrate his new ability, and he readily agrees. He stares at my third eye for only a few seconds and then his eyes go out of focus, and he begins describing my past lives, one after another, in rapid succession. In twenty of the past lives I am a male—in one I am Chinese—and in two of the past lives I am a female. To my utter stupefaction, he tells me I died of asthma in my last life. Whether he has read about my asthma in my clinic file, I have no way of knowing.

When I speak to Dr. Chow in his office about Joseph's newfound talent, his response is: "Need proof."

"But can chi kung give you the ability to see past lives?" I ask.

"Have this theory in religious chi kung, but I only teach medical chi kung." Trying to probe his belief system again, I ask him if we knew each other in a past life. "Only this life important," he says and then he taps on the glass wall of his office, summoning a patient from the waiting room.

Tripping the Chi
Fantastic

A patient of the clinic—a middle-aged woman with bad knees—has invited Dr. Chow to a dance, to be held in one of those old Legion Halls that still huddles on side streets in cities across North America. To my astonishment, the doctor accepts the invitation, but on the sole condition that I accompany him. Not without some hesitancy do I agree to be his wing man, uncertain as I am of the protocol expected of an apprentice. Am I supposed to scout out women for him at the dance? nudge him with good fellow camaraderie? exchange light party banter? "Try the artichoke dip, Dr. Chow. What flavor!"

The night of the dance, he is sitting in the passenger seat of my car, wearing a short leather coat over a pressed white shirt and gray flannels, and it is oddly disconcerting seeing the doctor out of his customary uniform. With the excited eyes of a teenager, he takes in the passing sights and points out items of interest.

In a conversational mood, the doctor wants to know what my thoughts are on the ideal mate. I tell him the ideal mate would be intelligent, compassionate, physically attractive, have a good sense of humor, share common interests, and have some kind of talent.

"Talent—this not for everybody. This only for you," he says.

"Yes, this only for me," I say.

"And you miss two important quality," he says.

"What are they?"

"Can cook—this important. And also, must be a clean person." A clean person who also knows how to cook—who could argue the point?

We arrive at the Legion Hall, and the bouncer at the club strikes out a thick arm barring the entranceway. He tells me I cannot enter because of my jeans. Appearing at that moment is the middle-aged patient with the bad knees. She talks to the bouncer in hushed tones. She then pulls away abruptly and struts to a phone booth at the corner. Five minutes later, a young man arrives in a car with a pair of brown corduroys hanging out the driver's window. In the backseat of the car I tug on the corduroys, which swamp my hips and creep up my calves like a pair of capris. But these are corduroys whose intrinsic pantness commands respect, and when I present myself to the bouncer once again, his large carnal face loosens, and he waves me inside.

Out of conservation or neglect, the Legion Hall has kept its linoleum floor from the fifties, with a striped pattern that decades of foot-polishing have worn down to a few black marks scattered across the surface like random exclamation points. At long wooden tables men and women are sitting in clusters, smoking cigarettes and talking over plastic cups while Hank Williams twangs from tinny speakers in every corner of the room.

If Dr. Chow is experiencing culture shock, he has nothing on me. The only person close to my age is the daughter of the middle-aged patient, and the daughter, twitching with boredom, asks me to dance before I even sit down. We are on our feet no more than two minutes when across the linoleum I spy Dr. Chow dancing with the middle-aged patient whose bad knees have acquired a new bounce. I find myself studying Dr. Chow's dance moves and wondering at their familiarity until I realize he is mirroring my own. As if to reveal he knows my thoughts, the doctor's face breaks into a wide smile. By the next song he has departed from my limited repertoire and is free styling his way across the floor, his dance partner boinging after him like a human pogo stick. Dr. Chow is a fabulous dancer, and now the whole attention of the room swings towards him.

For no reason that I can fathom, I am suddenly feeling very happy. When I turn my attention inward, I feel a stirring warmth rising from deep inside my belly and then the energy climbs higher into my body and into my face. I shoot a glance over at Dr. Chow. He is grinning in my direction. From a distance of twenty paces he is flicking chi at me with his fingertips. As the chi pings against my body, I begin to feel lighter and lighter—so much lighter, in fact, that if my feet were to leave the floor, I would not be surprised. I think of the legendary rabbis who would tether their feet in the presence of the Ark of the Covenant lest they fly skyward. I think of the great Tibetan yogi Milarepa who soared through the air on the wings of his joy. I think of the mystical golfer Shivas Iron in Michael Murphy's *Golf and the Kingdom* who spoke of suspending the laws of gravity.

There is a tap on my shoulder, and I whirl around. Dr. Chow has glided over like a ballroom dancer, and now he gives me a slap on the back that fires a bolt of chi deep within me. Twice more he slaps my back, and twice more the chi shoots through me like arrows of hot light.

At midnight we leave the Legion. We have just been invited to an after-party at the patient's house. As our car nibbles along a narrow residential street, I ask the doctor if dancing chi kung is something he learned in China, and he says dancing chi kung occurs naturally when you let the chi move freely about your body. I describe to him how light my body felt on the dance floor, and he says there is a term for this—*ching kung*. He says he is pleased at my sensitivity and that it bodes well for the big test. Before I can query him about the big test, he launches into a discussion about *ching kung* masters. These masters can walk on egg shells, he says, and they have been known to run along eaves-troughs and even telephone wires. Shortly after the Cultural Revolution ended, he says, one of these masters raced across a telephone wire and was shot dead by a guard who thought he was a spy. I tell him that what he has described is right out of a martial arts movie.

We park down the street from the house, and Dr. Chow takes up the subject of martial artists. Most of them acquire good kung fu through practice, he explains, but their kung fu is external, not internal, and so they age fast. But the greatest martial artists are like magicians, he says. They can stop someone dead in their tracks just by throwing chi to a certain point in their opponent's body. But if they do this too frequently, he adds, they will exhaust themselves. Even masters, he says, can deplete their chi to dangerous levels if they are not careful.

We walk toward the house, and suddenly he pauses in his tracks to tell me a story. A few years ago, he says, there was a chi kung master in Shanghai who scattered his chi to spectators in public demonstrations. The spectators were delighted by the gift, he says, but sometimes it is better to receive than to give. The Shanghai master gave away all his chi and died young.

Dr. Chow begins walking again, at a fast clip this time, and I hurry to catch up. He is twice my age and twice the athlete. I am curious to know how throwing chi could result in a master's death, and I put the question to him. Dr. Chow keeps walking, his eyes traveling around the neighborhood. If a master gives away a large quantity of chi, he says, he will dip into his original chi—his *yuan* chi, the chi he was born with. When this original chi is tapped out, he says, the master will die. It is the equivalent, he explains, of working yourself to death.

"But wouldn't a chi kung master know if he were dipping into his reserves?"

"Only traditional Chinese doctor know for certain. And most chi kung master not doctor."

"Aren't you two coming inside?" Our hostess, the middle-aged patient, is blocking the light of an open doorway. "Come in! Come in!" As we step inside the house, an elderly woman approaches Dr. Chow and asks what his first name is. When Dr. Chow replies that it is "Xiue"—pronounced Sue—the elderly woman grips his arm, exclaiming that she has a daughter named Sue, and what an incredible coincidence that is. Dr. Chow allows that it is indeed a coincidence, and as she releases his arm, she unfurls Sue's life like a scroll, beginning with Sue's breach birth fifty-one years ago.

Into our midst the middle-aged patient reaches her hand and draws the doctor aside, not to rescue him from an eternity of banality, but to confide in him her latest medical problem—a migraine headache. Dr. Chow guides her to a chair in a corner of the room, and there he holds his hands around her head, and lo, one minute later, the migraine goes away. But the middle-aged patient has one more favor to ask. Would Dr. Chow go upstairs and take a look at her four-year-old niece and come back with a prediction as to her future? He would not.

"Why?" asks the patient. He does not give predictions, he says.

"But I would be so happy if you did," says the patient imploringly. He understands, he says, but he is a doctor, not a professional psychic.

On the way home I glance over to the passenger seat and notice that Dr. Chow is clenching his fists together. His eyelids are almost shut, and the rising and falling of his chest is barely perceptible. As if feeling my gaze, he turns to me and opens his eyes. "This another way to generate chi," he says. "Use when you cannot do normal practice." Maybe it is the lateness of the hour, or maybe it is all the chi roiling around in my body, or maybe it is knowing these private moments will end some day, but I tell him it is a privilege to study under him. He laughs a little laugh to deflect the compliment, pats my hand, and says something in Chinese. When I ask what it means, he says, "Peter good student."

Chinese Brain, Chinese Face

I stare at my reflection in the bathroom mirror, and my eyes stretch wide. A coarse strand of jet-black hair has infiltrated a hank of blond hair at the front of my scalp. In Dr. Chow's office I point out the bold intruder, and immediately he rises from his chair, fetches a pair of surgical scissors, and holding the hair, snips it off. "This my hair," he says in explanation as he tapes the hair to a piece of paper.

"Your hair?" I ask. "What's it doing in my head?" Dr. Chow laughs and explains that when he throws his chi, he sends not only his energy, but his nutrition, which, coming from his body, contains certain information about his essence. He says I should find a lab to test the hair and see how it compares to the hair in his head. He goes on to say that having one of his hairs in my head also means that my brain is receiving his chi, and that means I am getting a new brain.

"A new brain?" I ask. Despite my apprehension I have to laugh.

"A Chinese brain," he says with immense simplicity. "This help you with big test." He goes on to say that encoded within his chi is the Chinese way of thinking, and so over time my brain will change. I thank him for the gift of his celebrated chi, but inform him politely that I am quite happy with my Western brain.

"Oh, you not lose Western brain. Just gain Chinese brain."

"But what if I don't want a Chinese brain?"

"Oh, this too late. Already have one. Didn't notice?" Notice I did. For weeks, for months, ideas have blown into my brain in great gusts of inspiration. Since I am making my living as a writer for television, my new flexible brain is a godsend. But should I attribute my new brain to the doctor's chi?

"Well, I do like fortune cookies now, and I never did before," I tell him.

Dr. Chow rubs his jaw and ponders the lot of the lowly fortune cookie. "This strange cookie. In China, never find this strange cookie. In Hong Kong, can find. But this Western invention. But now some Chinese also like this cookie." He leans back with narrowing eyes and gazes at my face. "Peter also get Chinese face."

I have to put a stop to this. "No, Dr. Chow. No Chinese face. Chinese brain, okay, but no Chinese face."

"Chinese face, you no like?"

"On you I like Chinese face." He slaps his knee and pitches his voice higher. "Peter's friends no recognize! I must take back all my chi so Peter can lose Chinese face! So much trouble you cause me!" He shakes a reproachful finger.

If becoming Chinese is one of the perks of receiving his chi, then why not a rapid improvement in my chi kung practice as well? I put the question to him, and in response he reaches over to a struggling plant on the floor and pretends to lift it from the top. "If you want plant to grow, and you do like this, then roots come out. No good." He slides his voice down three octaves for the proper gravitas. "What most important," he says, "is practice with big ambition. And no expect quick result."

"In that case, should I come to the clinic twice a day? In preparation for the big test?"

He shakes his head. "Of course big test important, but more important is you not become too dependent." His response brings to mind an aphorism in the *Tao Te Ching*. "When people no longer trust themselves, they seek a figure of authority. Therefore the Master steps back so that people won't become dependent and confused."

Dr. Chow stands up suddenly and tells me to go practice, needlessly pointing to the rooms down the hall. Traveling down the carpeted hallway, I hear his voice—he is singing, his voice floating on the air in a delicate warble. I am not knowledgeable about Chinese opera, but it is my belief that his voice could have won him fame and fortune on the opera circuit in China. The mind and hand of the doctor might be scientific, but not his voice. It soars.

When I emerge from the room half an hour later, Dr. Chow pushes me inside the bathroom, flicks on the light, and follows me wildly inside. "Look at your face!" he cries. It is not the same face I saw in the mirror this morning, nor glimpsed in the tailor's mirror before entering the clinic. It is not a Chinese face either, but it is entirely different from the one I know. This face glows with youth and vigor. "Go home, take picture with camera! Today, give you lots of chi!"

Leaving the clinic, I glance in the window of the hair salon next door. A decades-old photograph of a model is perched on a small wooden stand, her perfect hair in a coiffured flip, her perfect teeth set in a perfect smile for all the ages. Time's unravished bride, the model will remain young forever, but her photograph is in the wrong window.

Shanghai Mind-Meld

It is midnight. I have just finished my practice, and my whole body is sparkling. When I go to bed, I fall into a deep sleep almost immediately. About three in the morning I get up and go to the bathroom. Returning to the bedroom, I think to myself that Dr. Chow may be a remarkable teacher, but what are the limits of his powers? As a lark, I send him a telepathic message. "Since you're so accomplished, Dr. Chow, why don't you send me some chi right this minute?"

Before I have even crossed to the bed, I feel an electric jolt. I stand utterly still, my brain unnerved, my heart racing as a river of chi pours down my face and throat. After drawing a deep breath I consider the situation from a rational perspective. How could anyone hear my thoughts uttered silently at three in the morning—let alone respond to them with a blast of energy? The lunacy of the idea makes me smile, and the shouting headline of a tabloid pinwheels before my eyes: CHI KUNG MASTER TELEPATHIC! APPRENTICE THROWS AWAY PHONE!

In the clinic the next day I casually mention to Dr. Chow that I received some unexpected chi when I was thinking of him in the night, but he does not look up from his paperwork and instead responds in a muttering breath: "Go room, practice." A wave of relief passes over me. No salutation passed between teacher and student in the middle of the night. To think otherwise, I now realize, was to endow him with abilities he does not possess. The experience of the previous night I relegate to the residue of an overactive imagination, or something I ate for dinner. "An undigested bit of beef," as Scrooge says in *A Christmas Carol*, "a blot of mustard, a crumb of cheese, a fragment of an underdone potato."

The bulk of the month I spend at Toronto's Metropolitan Public Library where I am writing a screenplay on shamanism. One of my research books describes the practice of shamanism among the Lapps. The author of the book is not familiar with the concept of chi, but he describes how the Lapps used to playfully lash their children with birch twigs to transfer the life force trapped inside. As I read on, a vagrant thought swims into my mind, and it has nothing to do with the book I am reading. The thought expresses itself in an accented voice that I recognize as belonging to Dr. Chow, and the message is emphatic: *Peter, come to clinic early!*

A vague agitation moves in my body, and I return to my reading, the thought no longer present. But not less than five minutes later the thought reappears: *Peter, come to clinic early!* It seems strange that such a thought should come into my head. I have no desire to leave the library early. For the last couple of months I have gone to the clinic at around 6:30, which marks the end of my work day. And with fewer patients in the clinic, Dr. Chow often has a moment to chat. Once again I push the thought out of my mind and resume reading.

Only a few seconds pass before the thought returns once more. This is altogether too bewildering, and so I bookmark my page and try to compose myself, but no composure comes to my rattled brain, only a question. What if this message is not my own invention, but comes by way of his great craft? As if in response, the thought resounds in my head, the volume cranked up to a feverish pitch. *Peter, come to clinic early!* It is enough, amply enough. I will go to the clinic early.

When I arrive at 4:30, the light is out in the waiting room. I waltz inside, and as my eyes adjust to the darkness, I discover Dr. Chow standing at the entrance to the hallway, his hands thrust in his coat pockets. I school my voice to nonchalance and breezily announce that I got his message, and so here I am. He does not rebuke my levity, but neither does he affirm that he knows anything about a message. Instead, his response is immediate and startling. "Go inside, practice chi kung. Clinic close early today."

Some day in the future, when the phenomenon of telepathy is no longer explained away by coincidence or synchronicity, and accepted not just by parapsychologists, but by the entire scientific community, there will be a philosopher—perhaps from the Continent—who will muse on how the very existence of telepathy challenges our notion of privacy.

What was it that Wittgenstein said about the private language in our heads? (And what is the point of reading Wittgenstein in the first place unless you can reference him on occasion?) Wittgenstein said the private language in our heads depends on the existence of the public and social world. He said the language in your head is not *your* language, but *our* language, a language we all share. In this way Wittgenstein refuted solipsism. But I prefer this refutation of solipsism: knowing that a person can directly contact the mind of another.

In everything the purpose must weigh with the folly.

—*Henry IV, Part II*

Soren Kierkegaard and the Voice

Position yourself on the sidewalk at 545 St. Clair Avenue West, and tilt your head back. Now unfocus your eyes, and look through your eyelashes. Continue looking until Canada Chi Kung Health Clinic blurs into a new sign: Toronto School for the Magickal Arts.In magic schools of storybook legend, objects dart through the air. In the Toronto school, magical things fly through the air too, but the magic also moves inside you. When the inside-magic is running spitting-hot through your meridian cables and bits of light are flying in your body in all directions like sparks from a knife-sharpener's wheel, and when there are bursts of electrical fire in remote areas of your body and great flaming rivers are rushing up your spine and down your chest, and when there are sudden downsweeps and upsweeps of bubbling lava along your arms and legs and your brain-pan is a hot skillet, then every atom in your body pulses to the same rhythm, the pulsing rhythm of chi.

With my mind's eye I could observe the chi as it forged new pathways in my brain or traced circles of bright light around my heart or liver. But whom could I talk to about my inner sojourns? According to orthodox psychiatrists, if your description of the world runs counter to the accepted description of reality, then, by definition, you are psychotic. But my peculiar form of madness was not a breakdown—it was a breakthrough, as R. D. Laing would say.

Dr. Chow would nod at my rhapsodic accounts with polite understanding, but rarely countered with descriptions of his own experiences and never played the role of boon companion—how could a professor confer meaningfully with a kindergarten student? I did not wish to impose my experiences on my normal friends and have them think of me as strange, as not like themselves. I felt a hazy kinship with a friend who dropped acid once a month. And I felt a moment of shared epiphany with a long-beard I met by chance who had just returned from a solo canoe trip in the Canadian hinterland with eyes that had seen God. If my friend Joseph were still around, he would have been a good sounding board, but he had disappeared into the groves of academe, and I could not reach him. I could have relayed my experiences to other chi kung students, but I did not want to engender any competition. Too many students in the healing arts use their experiences to count coup—"You mean you haven't seen your aura yet? I change the color of my aura every day!"

In one respect, if in no other, I began to feel I had something in common with the Danish philosopher Soren Kierkegaard. In public, Kierkegaard played the role of a man about town and preached a gospel of worldliness, but in private he toiled over his philosophical works and told no one of his interior life. A popular fixture among his social set, he always kept himself apart psychologically. Even his books he published under a pseudonym to keep his two identities separate. But in his confessional autobiography, *The Point of View for My Work as an Author*, he finally made a clean breast of his double life. And in this book he declared that "the crowd is a lie, the crowd is an untruth." No witness for the truth "dare become engaged with the crowd."

Like Kierkegaard, I too chose to wear the mask of public acceptance. During the day I was occupied with my television writing, and at night I was a bon vivant. But unlike Kierkegaard, I was much taken by the crowd. To move out of meditative solipsism and be a saunterer among humanity—that was a siren call for me.

I was in my twenties, and I loved the winter cocktail parties with subtle flirtations made one night and forgotten the next, loved the spring dinner parties sparkling with smart commentary, loved the summer dances lit by the pink August sun. Soft autumn evenings led me along College Street with its Italian bars and cafes. With the changing taste of the air came changing colors in the trees and changing faces in the streets. New excitements urged me on, and I would be eager to get to the light and company of others. When there was frolic afoot, I would join a group of revelers strung along the sidewalk and follow their wanderings to bars with names like My Apartment or The Living Room or Peter's Backyard. Many a night I would have continued my nocturnal rambles and hailed in the dawn, but there was always the problem of the voice. The voice told me to be sensible. The voice told me to conserve my chi.

There are dogs who know when their keepers are coming home. And there are chi kung masters who know when their students are not coming home. On hearing the voice in my head, my mind would glide back restfully to my bedroom, my car would turn around like a pony ready to be stabled, and I would head home, still exultant and bursting with energy.

But some nights I did not head home. The voice might belong to Dr. Chow, but much better to ascribe it to my conscience so I could flout its monkish dictates if the night were truly magical, so I could once again be Kierkegaard's man of the world, so I could join the high-keyed laughter of the crowd and float along the city streets for one more glittering hour, until that hour became the eleventh hour of my conscience, until guilt, which prompts repentance, would guide me home again.

The Magic Wand

Made from onyx, jade, and marble, the wand is about four inches long and has a quartz crystal on the pointing end. The wand is sealed in a plastic bag and is the birthday gift of Megan, a fellow chi kung student. I am sitting in the clinic waiting room, about to open the plastic bag, when my friend angles her head in the direction of Dr. Chow's office. In a confidential voice she whispers that Dr. Chow has charged up the wand for me. My heart stands still with delight. A dream of childhood buried in childhood has just been exhumed and made real. *I am Mr. Wizard. I have a magic wand.*

Slowly I open the plastic bag and dip my hand inside. Immediately my hand feels electrified—as if I have immersed it in a soupy swirl of Victorian ectoplasm. As I pull the wand out, hairs lift on my arm. My friend leans forward with swelling enthusiasm but then two taps resound on the office window, and I put the wand back in the plastic bag. Forsaking the ease of the couch, I go to the office for my post-acupuncture pulse check.

Taking a seat in the patient's chair, I thank Dr. Chow for charging up the wand, and he grins shyly. I ask how long the wand's charge will last, and he says about a year. I ask what I can use the wand for, and with an amused face he says I can use it to heal a minor injury or illness. He takes the plastic bag from my hand, removes the wand, and makes a quick tight circle in the air. "This way release the chi."

"Why don't you ever use a wand yourself?" I ask. He drops the wand back into the plastic bag, seals it shut, and tells me the power will last longer this way. "Why don't you ever use a wand yourself?" I ask again. He looks at me with thoughtful reflection.

"My body is a wand. And my mind is a wand."

My body is a wand. And my mind is a wand.

Young children believe they can manipulate the external world with their thoughts, a state of mind Freud called the primary process. Psychologists will tell you this type of thought process is narcissistic, a type of magical thinking that can still be seen in many of the rituals of traditional cultures. It is also a type of mystical narcissism that is rife today among chronic positive thinkers and practitioners of wishcraft—just imagine it, and it will happen!

Instead of viewing magical thinking as simply another developmental stage in the human psyche, I like to think of it as a vestigal remnant of a time in human history when extraordinary powers were not the exclusive domain of a few individuals. But reclaiming our magical inheritance takes more than a seminar in a redwood forest or a month of repeating mantras of affirmation. Magical power relates directly to a person's ability to manipulate energy, because the power is not magical at all, but rather biophysical energy, which is part of the emerging science of the new millennium.

With my magic wand in my pocket, I go to a cafe to meet with Ted Mann, one of Dr. Chow's patients. I have told Ted about the wand, and he is anxious to test it out. Ted is not hard to pick out in a crowd with his wispy white beard and elfin features. Part merry prankster, part social scientist, he is one of the foremost authorities on Wilhelm Reich and shares Reich's fascination for energy of all kinds. As I approach his table, I notice a blue blanket on the chair beside him. "It's an orgone blanket," Ted explains, lifting it off the chair. "One of Reich's students designed it. Here, try it." I sit down and place the blanket over my knees. With my eyes closed against the bright glint of the afternoon, I turn my sight inwards.

"There's energy coming from this," I tell Ted, my eyes still shut. "But it's different from what I've experienced before. It seems coarser somehow." I open my eyes and ask what the blanket is composed of. Ted answers that it is three layers of steel wool. He adds that Wilhelm Reich thought the blanket had the potential to heal. He falls silent for a moment, then shifting lightly in his chair, asks with subdued eagerness if I have brought the magic wand. I nod slowly, and his eyes grow wide. Having a magic wand on your person is like having contraband. There is a subversive delight just knowing it is in your possession. I glance around the coffee shop. No one has the slightest interest in what we are doing. When I produce the plastic bag, Ted's mouth opens. I remove the wand, and he leans forward. Grasping his hand, I circle the wand's crystal tip around the center of his palm.

"It tingles!" he cries softly. Then, reaching across the table: "Can I hold it myself?" I give him the wand, and he studies it with intense interest. He twirls it over the back of his hand like a swizzle stick, and his breath comes short and sharp. Then he points the wand at his elbow and shakes the tip vigorously. I think to myself I have just lost a month's worth of wand chi in that single gesture, and Ted has not yet finished. He is tracing an invisible line between his elbow and palm and exclaiming about the sensation. Then he switches hands and moves the wand over his other arm, his face transfigured. More chi flies out of the crystal tip as he works it like a salt shaker over an injured finger. He is lost in the energy of the wand, and I pry it from his hand and hurry it back inside the plastic bag.

Three days later Ted calls me and reports in an excited voice that his finger is healed. Ted's healed finger is only the first of the wand's many successes. Some of my siblings are among the recipients of the wand's largesse. But the bulk of the treatments are given to my new girlfriend. Forever bumping into things, she asks for a wand-twirl three or four times a week. At one point I accuse her of being deliberately clumsy, and her face expresses genuine surprise.

After about thirteen months I retire the wand, its energy spent. A month later my girlfriend injures herself again, and I hunt around my office for it. But the wand has performed its last act of magic: it has disappeared.

My Girlfriend and Charles Dickens

I wake up one morning, and resting on the pillow beside me is a mystery—the rosy mystery of love. Mystery's name is Jenifer Lass, a sparkling beauty of high spirits and lovely friendliness who makes her living as an actress and model. Jenifer does not share my interest in Chinese medicine, but after reaping the benefits of the magic wand, is game enough to visit Dr. Chow as a patient. The acupuncture she finds reviving, but at home she slyly pours her steaming medicine into the houseplants, thinking I will not notice. And I notice nothing until the houseplants sprout luxuriant new growth and Jenifer owns up to her new fertilizing technique.

After being away from the clinic for a while, Jenifer is alarmed to learn from her Western doctor that she has developed an enlarged ovary. Her Western doctor wants her to have the ovary removed in a week's time, but Jenifer pays a visit to Dr.

Chow, and he urges her to try an herbal remedy first. I am appointed doctor-in-residence at chez Meech and charged with mixing powdered herbs with Chinese vinegar before applying the resulting paste at the site above the enlarged ovary. Five days later Jenifer's ovary has shrunk back to normal, and her Western doctor, astounded but delighted, cancels the operation.

Jenifer likes to refer to herself as a walking medical disaster, and twice more she has occasion to play guinea pig for the herbal paste. A month after her ovary heals, she fractures her tail-bone, and again I apply the paste. When a profusion of lumps appears in her breasts, I apply the paste once more. Jenifer recovers from both conditions. So impressed am I by the efficacy of the herbal paste that I ask Dr. Chow about its origin. "Herbs come from China," he says. When I press him further, he admits modestly, "This medicine I invent myself to help patient."

Though her health is fully restored, Jenifer does not abandon Chinese medicine altogether. Without her knowledge or consent she is becoming a chi kung student of sorts, by virtue of our close proximity. If I happen to practice chi kung next to her, she gets tingling sensations in her arms or legs. Because of her acute sensitivity to energy, she can tell if I am achieving a strong or weak result with my practice.

One night I am performing standing chi kung in a corner of the bedroom when Jenifer looks up from a book she is reading and asks if I was aware that Charles Dickens was a chi kung practitioner. She hands me Peter Ackyrod's biography, and I read the page she has earmarked. Evidently, Dickens was a strong believer in animal magnetism, and he believed he could use the power to heal others.

In a well-documented case that Ackyrod reports, Dickens both hypnotized and attempted to heal a woman by the name of Augusta de la Rue. A nervous disorder that manifested itself as a spasm on her face was the primary focus of his attention. He would give magnetic transmissions to his patient both in person and while on his frequent travels. While in Dickens's care, Augusta de la Rue did recover, although in later years her symptoms reappeared.

There was one incident in particular that convinced Dickens of his healing powers. While riding in a coach with his wife, he sent a burst of energy to his distant patient, with an unexpected side effect. According to Dickens, his energy field suddenly enveloped his wife, and she promptly fainted. Of course, the reaction of Dickens's wife could easily have been the result of her suggestibility, which Dickens did not take into account.

As I read the biography on the bed, I practice chi kung at the same time. Jenifer shivers suddenly, says she just felt a surge of energy in her stomach, and asks jokingly if I was sending chi to some mysterious patient a few miles away.

If Augusta de La Rue had ever witnessed Dickens transmit energy in the dark, she might have detected the same phenomenon that Jenifer did that evening. I am practicing the standing position in a corner of the bedroom when I hear Jenifer gasp. I spin around. Her eyes are wide with astonishment. In a shrieking voice she says that sparkles of white light are moving over my face and along my arms. I rush to the mirror, but all I can see is a dim outline of my features.

Another evening Jenifer observes colors on my body—flourescent green, purple, and blue. Sometimes the colors appear as small glowing patches, she says, and sometimes they blink on and off like slow-moving fireflies. Every time she identifies a color I rush to the mirror, but to me the colors always remain elusive.

Over time Jenifer's sensitivity to chi increases, and she begins having dreams of future events in her life—a phone-call from a childhood friend not heard from in years, a surprise job offering, the unexpected pregnancy of a friend. The dreams come true, but there is one that does not come true—that she will fall and break her leg while crossing the street. On the day the accident is to occur, she takes precautions and manages to avoid disaster.

One night I come home very late and find Jenifer asleep in bed. In the morning she tells me of an unusual occurrence that took place while I was out. She was in a dead sleep when she bolted awake suddenly. There was a presence in the room, she says, but it was benevolent and did not frighten her. Within seconds, she felt an intense heat around her knee, which she had injured the previous week. The heat spread around the injured area and penetrated to the bone. A moment later she sensed a change of energy in the room—the presence had departed—and, overcome with drowsiness, she drifted back to sleep. As she relays the story to me, Jenifer speaks with utter conviction that what she experienced was not a dream. I ask about the present condition of her knee, and she replies that it feels much better.

When I venture into Dr. Chow's office later that day, he asks what I was doing the previous night. I tell him I was playing chess, at which point his face draws closer and he taps a finger on the table in gentle reproof. Playing chess, he says, takes energy. Playing chess well, he says, takes a great deal of energy. I assure him I am a player of limited skill, and then I ask him what he was doing last night. He gives me a coy look, and I repeat the question.

"Visit Peter in bedroom," he says finally, "but Peter no there." With a shy smile he adds, "So give Jenifer chi instead."

Mainstream science asserts that out-of-body experiences are really a misperception of the brain. Countering this assertion are thousands of personal anecdotes, the studies of some parapsychologists, and the accounts found in religious literature and occult lore. If someday it is proven that people can actually leave their bodies, mainstream science will undergo a paradigm shift. But leaving your body is one thing. Directing your astral body to a specific location and then throwing energy? This will always be the stuff of science-fiction. Or will it?

It is a pleasant and perfect day, and I am treading soft-footed through the soft grass of the park. As I give pasture to the thought of energy transmission from the astral state, I become elated, bewildered. Then my mind drops away from the utter strangeness of it all, and I let my eyes play among the leaves of the trees.

*The invisible forces acting in the visible body can be
guided by the imagination and propelled by the will.*

—Franz Anton Mesmer

The Mesmerizing
Mr. Mesmer

Chi kung masters, yogis, sorcerers, shamans—I want to learn about their experiences to gain insight into my own, and so as my chi kung apprenticeship progresses, I embark on a course of intensive reading. Maybe, I tell myself, I will learn something that will give me insight into the big test. Dr. Chow has not mentioned the big test for some time, and I have not brought it up. I live with the vague hope that he has forgotten it.

I am reading *Zen and the Art of Archery* in the waiting room when Dr. Chow walks over and asks me what the story is about. I tell him it is autobiographical and concerns a German university professor—Eugene Herrigel—who apprenticed himself to an archer in Japan. I tell him this archer, a Zen monk, taught Herrigel a breathing technique that resulted in a spiritual power flowing through Herrigel's arms and legs. This spiritual power was chi (spelled *ki* in the book), and it enabled Herrigel to draw back the large Japanese bowstring and become an archer himself.

The story delights Dr. Chow, and I begin bringing other books into the clinic that I think he will enjoy discussing. My brief synopses of the books gives him the opportunity to wax philosophical, and our end-of-day discussions add a philosophical note to the apprenticeship. One evening we discuss two 20th century French philosophers—Bergson and Merleau-Ponty—both of whom proposed theories of the body that have similarities to the meridian system. Dr. Chow correctly observes that neither Bergson nor Merleau-Ponty knew the art of cultivating his own life-energy and so had only limited knowledge of what life-energy is capable of. Another evening we discuss Wilhelm Reich and his concept of orgone energy. Dr. Chow agrees that orgone energy bears a striking resemblance to chi. But of all the remarkable individuals who come under Dr. Chow's scrutiny, it is Mesmer—an 18th century physician from Lake Constance—who intrigues him the most.

Born in 1734, Mesmer grew up to become a respected physician in Vienna before he was marginalized by the medical community by publicly declaring that magnets could be used for healing. A few years later, at the age of thirty-two, he realized the magnetic potential of his own body, and he gave away all his magnets and began transferring his own life-energy—he called it *fluidium*—to his patients. Known today as the father of hypnotism, Mesmer has been largely misinterpreted. Most modern-day psychologists who are interested in Mesmer's work subscribe to the notion that he unwittingly hypnotized his patients—mesmerized them—as a result of his astounding rapport. In other words, Mesmer's patients cured themselves of their ailments through the placebo effect, or so the theory goes.

Mesmer was well aware of the power of suggestion. He knew that the force of his personality, combined with the soothing ambience of the clinic, contributed to the success of his cures.

Yet he always maintained that at the base of his cures was the transmission of life-energy. And he was quick to dispel any notion that he himself possessed any kind of supernatural power. Time and again he stated that he had simply learned how to tap into a universal energy and that anyone could do it with proper training. To prove his point, he trained apprentices who later carried on his work.

As I talk about Mesmer one evening in the clinic office, Dr. Chow sits back in his chair and listens with curious eyes. He wonders aloud if Mesmer could have been a chi kung master, and I tell him about Mesmer's monumental work: *Memoire de Monsieur Mesmer Sur La Decoverte du Magnetisme Animal.* In his book Mesmer states that just as a magnet has two opposing poles, so does the human body. I ask Dr. Chow what he thinks of this proposition, and he says it is correct. The crown on the head (*bai hui*) is yang, he says, and the perineum point (*hui yin*) in the pubic region is yin. Then he raises his hands and says the left is yang, the right is yin. He says there are many examples of magnetic duality throughout the body.

He asks what abilities Mesmer had as a healer, and I describe to him a classic experiment that took place one afternoon in Mesmer's house. To test the theory of animal magnetism, Mesmer invited a physician from the Royal Academy of London to his house. Following Mesmer's instructions, the physician touched the arm of a comatose patient lying behind a screen. The patient—a young woman—gave no response to the touch. Mesmer then rubbed both of the physician's hands and instructed him to touch the patient again. When the physician made contact with the patient this time, her body rippled in small convulsions. Another contact by the physician and then another, and on each occasion the patient exhibited the same reaction.

Dr. Chow raises his hand to interrupt and says everything I described could have been faked by the patient. I agree, but I tell him there is more to the story. I then describe the other experiments Mesmer conducted with the physician. In one of these experiments, Mesmer brought out several china cups from the kitchen and told the physician to choose one, after which Mesmer passed his hands over the chosen cup and magnetized it. The physician took the other unmagnetized cups and, one by one, passed them over the surface of the patient's body with no result. When he repeated the same action with the magnetized cup, a visible shudder ran down the length of the patient's body.

Dr. Chow nods for me to continue, and I tell him how Mesmer then took the physician's hands in his and with great concentration transmitted energy into the physician's own body. At Mesmer's behest the physician then touched one of the cups himself, crossed over to the patient and passed the cup over her body, causing her body to shake. A moment later the physician repeated the procedure with the unmagnetized cups, but the patient had no reaction. And there was still one experiment remaining. Eight yards from the patient and giving no verbal or physical cues, Mesmer sent a steady stream of energy through his finger, and immediately the patient's body began to shake. Then Mesmer positioned the physician between the patient and himself and again pointed his finger. Once again the patient's reaction was nothing short of dramatic.

Listening to the story, Dr. Chow inclines his head forward. All these effects, he says quickly, could be accomplished by a chi kung master, but he warns that trickery has always existed in the field of chi kung, and a person must remain on the lookout. He lowers his voice even though we are alone in the clinic. He says there are many chi kung masters today who are nothing more than persuasive con men.

I ask if it is possible to magnetize any kind of object as Mesmer claimed, and Dr. Chow says it is. I tell him that patients in Mesmer's clinic would eat from magnetized plates, wear magnetized clothes, read magnetized books, and drink magnetized water. Dr. Chow laughs with his full body, and suddenly it occurs to me that he might be laughing out of sympathy. Is not the very chair I am sitting on saturated with chi? Is not the very desk I am resting my elbows upon saturated with chi? Is not the very air I am breathing in his office saturated with chi? I recall the time when an elderly man walked into the waiting room of the clinic and began crying. He said he was extremely sensitive to energy fields and that the energy in the waiting room—*the waiting room*—had overwhelmed him.

I tell Dr. Chow that Mesmer thought that universal energy could not only be communicated, but propagated and intensified by sounds, that this energy could be stored up, concentrated and transported, and that this energy was intensified and reflected by mirrors, just like light. As Dr. Chow listens to the propositions, he nods continuously in agreement. Then I describe Mesmer's invention that brought him fame and ridicule across Europe—the baquet.

Dr. Chow hands me a pencil and paper and asks me to draw a picture of a baquet, and I make a crude sketch of a round tub with a bottom layer of pulverized glass sprinkled with iron fillings. Then I draw a second layer arrayed with bottles of water. The glass, the iron fillings, and the bottled water, I explain, were magnetized by Mesmer. I add that he sometimes filled the entire tub with magnetized water. Finishing the drawing, I sketch a round lid with curving rods of iron protruding from several holes. I explain that the patients gripped the iron rods, through which flowed the healing energy. Dr. Chow shakes his head at the ingenuity of it all.

Then I tell the doctor about the famous tree on Mesmer's estate that Mesmer occasionally used in his healing ceremonies. The species of tree was unknown, but it was said to retain its leaves until early winter and to produce leaves in the early spring before any other tree in the area. Dr. Chow listens with a smiling intensity, but offers no comment, and so I put the question to him directly: Could a chi kung master throw chi to a tree and transform it into a chi-delivery system for patients?

Dr. Chow's mind lights at once upon the essentials. Thrusting forth his head, he speaks in rapid sentences. Any tree, he says, would give off a certain amount of chi—hence, a patient would receive some benefit just by being nearby. And if the master threw chi to a tree to which the patient was connected, then yes, the patient would get a boost of chi from the tree. If the master did this frequently enough, then the tree itself would flourish along with the surrounding vegetation. If the master were present when the patient was standing by the tree, several things would have to be taken into consideration. Was the master throwing his chi secretly to the patient? Or was he not throwing chi at all—to the patient or the tree? If the master were strong enough, the patient could be receiving his chi just by being in his energy field. Then again, the patient, if suggestible, might himself be responsible for the healing—in other words, the placebo effect. Or the patient could be misreporting the result, based on an erroneous belief in the efficacy of the treatment or to please the master.

As I leave the clinic that night, I consider how Dr. Chow's detailed response reveals his scientific bent of mind. And I wonder about the observations of my own chi. Have I ever misreported the results of my practice to please the doctor, imagining effects that did not take place?

A Hospital Visit

When we arrive at the Toronto General Hospital, I pull up to the curb, but Dr. Chow remains in his seat.

"Better you find parking space," he says, rumbling his deep voice. "And follow me." Am I to help heal a patient? Or just observe the doctor at work? I want to ask what he has in mind for me, but he seems preoccupied, his brow clouded with worry. Past a security desk, up an elevator, down a hospital corridor we travel. As we stride toward a patient's room, I speak to him in an undertone.

"The hospital lets you practice here?"

"Patient ask me come here."

From outside the patient's room we hear a woman's voice screaming shrill invective. Dr. Chow swings open the door as the owner of the voice—a man, not a woman—continues the rant. The man weighs less than one hundred pounds and is dressed in pajamas that engulf his shrunken frame. His venomous rage is directed toward two women in a corner who listen with weary abstraction. As Dr. Chow advances into the room, the patient looks abashed. In a voice winnowed of all vigor he says, "Thank you for coming, Dr. Chow."

"How you feeling?" asks Dr. Chow in a soft voice.

"Like a million bucks!" the patient cries. "Why do you think I called you here!" This last effort costs him dearly, and he coughs hard.

"No shout," says Dr. Chow gently. "Save energy."

The patient strains his head to look at me and then breaks into a smile. Pursing his lips together, he says, "I predicted you would study with Dr. Chow. Am I a good psychic or what?" I notice the wraparound black sunlasses on the nightstand. I hide my surprise at the dramatic change in his physical appearance and give him a salute.

"You're an excellent psychic, Jerry." But Jerry has switched his gaze to the two women in the corner—one of whom apparently is his sister—and he begins shouting again, his voice stuck on one note.

"Jerry, be quiet!" says Dr. Chow, and Jerry is cowed into silence, his head sinking into the pillow.

"I give you treatment now," says Dr. Chow. "Shut your eyes." Jerry's eyelids drop down, and he takes one long sighing breath. The hands of Dr. Chow describe strange twisting movements and then his fingers pluck the air like a marionette artist. A welcome serenity passes over Jerry's features, and for a moment he has the blissful look of a gaunt medieval saint. The process of throwing chi lasts for about three minutes—longer than I have ever witnessed or experienced. The moment Dr. Chow finishes, Jerry's eyes flash open.

"You remember how practice chi kung?" Dr. Chow asks. Jerry's eyes are aflame, and he lifts his voice to an angry pitch.

"I can't feel my chi anymore! How do you expect me to practice it!"

"Must practice," Dr. Chow says in a commanding voice. "This I tell you as your doctor." Taking Jerry's pulse, Dr. Chow writes down an herbal prescription. Then he turns to Jerry's sister and says that if Jerry is to get better, he must drink the herbal medicine twice a day. Jerry begins screaming again at the two women with intense indignation, and so we fare out of the room without saying goodbye. At the threshold of the doorway I turn back for a moment and take a last look. A shiver runs through my body, and I step into the hallway with the breath sucked out of me.

On the main floor of the hospital Dr. Chow locates a public bathroom and excuses himself. From the hallway I can hear him clearing his throat again and again—I imagine him expelling whatever portion of Jerry's illness he acquired in the energy exchange. Long ago I noticed a habitual hock in the doctor's throat after treating a patient. I would hear him spit in the sink in his office, and I would surmise he was ridding himself of whatever pathogens his body had absorbed.

We head back to the clinic in my car, and I can tell by the doctor's focused demeanor that his expended energy is miraculously replacing itself. "Does Jerry have AIDS?" I ask.

"This not Chinese diagnosis. This Western diagnosis."

"Can he get better?"

"Can." His eyes shut suddenly, like blinds crashing down, and I ask no more questions.

A month later I am at the clinic for my daily chi kung session when Dr. Chow calls me into his office. His hands are holding his forehead, like a man trying to stop a bleeding wound. With a faltering voice he tells me that Jerry died an hour ago. A moment passes in silence.

"Maybe there was nothing you could do, Dr. Chow. Maybe it was too late."

"Wasn't too late," he says under his breath. He explains that Jerry had refused to drink the herbal medicine, and so the family had stopped giving it to him. But he says the family should not have reacted in this way. When a patient is on the brink of death and acts like a baby, you must treat the patient like a baby. You must plug his nose and pour the medicine down his throat.

"I liked Jerry," I say. Dr. Chow says nothing and touches the tips of his fingers to his eyelids.

The Throwing and Catching of Chi

"What's your feeling?" When Dr. Chow poses the question, I am still as a waxwork, my eyes shut, my hands hanging loose by my side. He has dimmed the lights in the room, and I turn my sight inwards.

"Pain," I say. "I feel pain. And pressure on the crown of my head. And a pulsing in my third eye region."

"Good," he says. There is a pause of about ten seconds. "Now—what's your feeling?"

Except for a trickling of chi around my head, I feel nothing. Could this be a test to see if I am imagining something? My doubts vanish the next moment as a swath of chi cuts down the center of my chest. Translating the sensation into chi-speak, I tell Dr. Chow the chi is traveling down the ren mei or ren channel.

"That's right," he says. My senses are on full alert. Ten more seconds, and he blurts out again, "Now—what's your feeling?" Again, there is a momentary delay before the chi reveals itself.

"My lower back, the ming men point. There's a sharp penetration. A hot stabbing needle."

"And now? What's your feeling now?" Where the chi alights this time is hard to determine. The energy from the other throws is diffusing around my body, and to distinguish between this diffusion and the location of the new throw is difficult. There are sensations everywhere, I tell him.

"Practice chi kung." He snaps off the overhead light, ending the day's strange catechism.

And so the game continues, day in and day out, for many weeks. These are small tests, Dr. Chow tells me, and I must pass them successfully before I can take the big test. It has been several months since Dr. Chow has mentioned the big test, and the thought of it still excites and unnerves me. I ask when he plans to administer the big test, and he replies that it depends on my progress. And my progress, he says, depends on my practice. Affecting an off-handed manner I ask if he can tell me any details about the big test, and he smiles. Part of the big test, he reminds me, is understanding the big test.

As the small tests continue there comes a time when Dr. Chow asks me not only the location of each throw, but the kind of chi he is throwing. Recently I have discovered that his chi has different shapes and textures. The chi can be light or heavy. It can hit my body in several places at once like hard drops of rain, or it can hit like a solid brick of energy. Sometimes it feels as if I have brushed against the branches of a pine tree. Sometimes the chi passes through my body in a succession of waves. Frequently I experience a light coating of chi that sinks deep into my bones like a penetrating balm. In one session a cloud of chi engulfs me, and I am floating inside a womb, suspended in a warm amniotic fluid.

During one of the testing periods my body begins to sway. Dr. Chow instructs me to let the chi roam where it will, and this means my feet will move on their own accord, because that is what they want to do. Gently, gently, one foot follows the other in a slow clockwise circle like the Frankenstein monster taking his first tottery steps. This slow-stepping circle becomes my established pattern until one day the direction of the chi changes, and I reverse my course. Every test thereafter, the chi changes direction at least once, sometimes several times in quick succession, and as my body becomes more sensitive I respond more quickly.

After a few months, a new game: I am waiting in the room for Dr. Chow, thinking he has forgotten about me, and so I call out. He appears a moment later, turns off the overhead light, and leaves. But he has not thrown any chi, and I am mystified. Before any time has passed, however, a shower of chi falls over my body like a warm summer rain. When I appear in his office afterward, he asks what time I felt the chi. I tell him it was just after he shut the door. He leans forward, planting both elbows on the desk. "What other time?" Suddenly I remember a hot flash of energy that streaked down the right side of my body about half way into the session. I tell him the approximate time of the throw, and he smiles."Peter got it."But the answer has opened up another question.

"Where did you throw it from?"

"Outside room. Don't remember me walking outside room?" I do remember hearing something outside the door, but it was a goblin step, a fairy footfall, and I thought nothing of it.

"So no problem throwing through a wall?" I ask.

"You catch better now, so this easy throw." I am reminded about what Joseph said about the big test—how one must be able to catch chi from a distance, and I am heartened.

Three months later. I am in the darkened room. I have been practicing standing chi kung for ten minutes when, from the ceiling, spiraling toward my head, comes a white blur. I blink my eyes. The blur is still spiraling toward my head. What am I to think? Is the white blur an optical illusion, or is it the result of my third eye opening?

My mind travels back a few weeks to an acupuncture session when Dr. Chow offered to open the chi kung point located at my third eye. While I lay on the examining table, he drew his face within three inches of mine and, clamping his fingers on my temples, pressed his thumbs on the bone between my eyebrows. I heard a cracking sound and felt a rhythmic pulsing, and then a wave of heat passed into my skull. The whole procedure lasted about fifteen seconds. Over time, said Dr. Chow, I would feel my third eye opening. He added that having the third eye open does not mean a person is enlightened, it just means the *shen* is strengthened. I had read about the shen in *The Yellow Emperor's Classic of Internal Medicine*, the ancient text from the Han Dynasty. According to the author of the text, the shen, or spirit, reveals itself when the heart is open and attentive and when the eyes are perceptive. But in Dr. Chow's lexicon, shen also refers to the supernatural powers emanating from the head. With good shen, not only are the powers of the third eye and mind strengthened, the powers of the eyes are strengthened too. Through the eyes, he said, one can send chi and do other amazing things.

My mind returns to the present and the darkened room I am standing in. The origin of the white blur mystifies me. Dr. Chow has not walked past my door once during this session. Later, when I report to Dr. Chow in his office, I ask him, point blank, at what point he threw his chi. He asks me why I want to know, and I tell him I am merely testing my sanity. A bemused expression appears on his face, and he says, "Ten minute after you go to room." I draw a deep breath and ask how he threw the chi to me, and he points a finger to the rectangular air duct on the ceiling above his desk.

"You threw it down the air duct?" He laughs modestly and nods his head. A shock passes through me, and it registers on my face.

"Oh, this just basic physics," he says. "Chi travel fast this way." Basic physics, I think to myself, does not concern itself with the remarkable person responsible for transmitting this remarkable energy.

I pause for a moment, marveling at his ability and then I say, "I think I saw your chi today."

"Isn't it?"

"Is it always white, your chi?"

"Chi have many colors."

"Can you tell me about the different colors?"

From the expression on his face I can tell his modesty is at odds with his desire to disclose the factual nature of his abilities. He solves the problem by talking about what Joseph has seen before. Joseph has seen a variety of different colors—primarily white, but sometimes gold, blue or green. Dr. Chow adds that the color he throws depends on a patient's condition and how much energy the patient's body can absorb. I tell him one of his students—a female—recently told me that he had thrown red chi.

"Red is color of anger," he says. "I never throw this one."

"This student also said that you throw different colors to different areas of the body at the same time."

"No, this student mistaken. Never happen like that. Always one color only." He goes on to say that students of chi kung imagine a great many things, which is why he tests and retests me to make sure I get things right. Then he draws closer as if to reveal a great mystery. "Chi is like light, but is different than light. Chi can bend."

The painters of old, using precise measurements of line and color, made us see with new eyes and feel with new hearts. How much like a great painter is this chi kung master who paints with equal precision, in brush strokes of light-energy. But his canvass is the human body, and he uses bending light of different colors.

It is not the viewer of this artwork who is changed, but the patient, the artwork itself.

The Hyena

Among his regular clientele Dr. Chow attracted not a few
camp followers, all of whom were women. There were the
Romantics whose secret crushes on the doctor were openly written on their faces. There were the Forlorn who lived on the
margins of life and sought only the doctor's comforting presence.
And then there were the Wheedlers who doled out flattery and
small gifts to the embarrassed doctor, hoping for that extra dol-
lop of chi. But the fateful day would come when the devoted
patient would attain perfect health, and on that day she would
leave the clinic with barely concealed dissatisfaction. And one
could imagine her visiting sick beds, buying damaged tins of
food, or searching out unsanitary restaurants in hopes of a speedy
relapse.

Of all the Wheedlers in the clinic the best by far was the
Hyena. She was never without a little lagniappe for the good doctor, accompanied by a smile so oily it could make one's digestion-
pulse drop ten points on the spot. I first heard her when she took
a seat opposite me in the waiting room. *Heard,* I say, because her

arms clanged with more bracelets than a Bedouin bride, and she was laughing about something with the mirthless laugh of a hyena. In a glance her eyes appraised me and found me wanting, and she swished her short red hair to one side. I went back to my magazine, but every few moments she would clang, and I would look up to see her touching the ends of her short red hair, which seemed to draw color from her red lacquered nails.

One day Dr. Chow introduced me to the Hyena as his long-time student, and suddenly, in her eyes, I was vaulted into an august realm, and thereafter she treated me with her first manner—always polite and effusively complimentary. I would be writing about my chi kung session in the waiting room, and she would sit beside me and deliver a string of compliments as a warm-up. Then she would drop her voice to a thoughtful tone, a tone I came to recognize as a warning she was about to share a confidence. In these private moments I learned she hailed from the Eastern seaboard of the United States, was independently wealthy, and had recently divorced for the fourth time. If I had one minute to spare, she would descant vigorously on all the famous people she had met that week and if I had two minutes to spare, all the famous people she had met that month. Over time I learned that her second manner—by which I mean her unrestrained scorn—was reserved for anyone who was not famous. For some unknown reason, students of chi kung escaped her reckoning.

As if to reassure herself that her investment in me was worthwhile, the Hyena would occasionally ask if Dr. Chow ever spoke about her. Since the doctor never discussed one chi kung student with another, I could offer her no insights. But I was as keenly interested in his opinion of her as she was. I wondered if he saw past her hard laughter, her blandishments and small trinkets presented to him with great ceremony or whether the complexities of her character were lost in cultural translation. I knew he could not be propitiated, but could he be conned? One day I got my answer, but not in the way I expected.

Dr. Chow waved me into his office, and as I lowered myself into the patient's chair, he fixed his eyes on mine. "What Peter dream about last night?"

"I never remember my dreams. Why do you ask?"

"Peter should pay attention to dreams."

"Why should Peter do this?"

"Because this help you with the big test." Once again, the mythical test had resurfaced. So much time had passed since its first mention that it was beginning to seem unreal.

"How will my dreams help me with the big test?"

"Must pay attention. Then you find out."

That night, for the first time in my life, I made a conscious effort to remember my dreams. Alert to the wanderings of my mind, I stayed awake for more than two hours until at last the world slipped away, and I fell into a deep sleep. A few hours later I woke up suddenly, and I recalled a vivid dream. In my dream I was standing before a giant white chart on which were listed my few good qualities and many shortcomings. Check marks in various columns indicated how much of a certain characteristic I possessed.

I remember running my finger along the chart and stopping at a column marked "Lazy." My mind flinched—the column contained more check marks than I cared to count. Then Dr. Chow appeared in his white lab coat and, without saying a word, directed my attention to a second chart. Somehow I knew the second chart belonged to the Hyena. There were several columns that listed her shortcomings, but there were columns that listed her good qualities too. One of the qualities listed was "help people," and this column contained many check marks. I considered that this column might be referring to her charity work, which I had overheard her discussing a day earlier. So Dr. Chow had seen through her after all, but seen through her in a way I had not.

In the morning the dream had lost none of its vividness. But Mercury, the Bringer of Dreams, is a trickster. Was the dream of my own making, or did Dr. Chow choreograph its contents? The idea that someone could enter another person's dreams through a simple act of volition...

I strode into the clinic and found Dr. Chow alone in his office. "Dr. Chow, I had a dream last night."

"Isn't it?" I gave him a few details about the two charts, about his mysterious appearance, but I did not discuss any of my personal deficits so thoroughly catalogued. "So you got it," he said. "This good."

"How difficult is it to get inside another person's dream?" I asked.

"How many million Chinese practice chi kung?" he asked. "If easy get inside person's dream, then everybody do it. But they no do it. So this not easy do." A feeling of unworthiness swept over me. How unfortunate for this great teacher to have chosen an apprentice as lazy as me. As I was leaving the office, he said: "Must continue practice harder. No lazy." I turned around quickly, and his eyes were sparkling.

A new phase in the apprenticeship had begun. Why Dr. Chow chose to teach through the medium of dreams, he never explained. In his own private calculus it must have made sense, or he would never have expended the tremendous energy it required. My own guess was he chose dream teaching for practical reasons. If a picture is worth a thousand words, then with each dream image he had a thousand less words with which to struggle.

A Jedi Knight

We slide past a frosty blur of glass and steel until we have left Toronto. Another hour passes, and we are traveling under the gray shroud that overhangs the city of Hamilton in the early winter, and then we coast into snow-speckled countryside. Buckled in beside me is Dr. Chow, and cradled in the backseat is Tamiyo. Though Tamiyo and I are no longer dating, we are still great friends.

For weeks Tamiyo has been telling Dr. Chow he should enlarge his knowledge of traditional medicine and meet an Indian medicine woman named Twyla Nitsch. And so it has finally come about that we are making the trek to a reservation in upper New York State. Earlier today, in preparation for the journey, Dr. Chow shucked off his white lab coat, slipped on his black leather jacket, and drank a cup of herbal tea—"special tea," he said, "for chi kung master."

The talk in the car has passed beyond pleasantries, and we have settled into a comfortable silence. Uncounted minutes slide by, and I feel no need to strike up a conversation, but I also know that having Dr. Chow trapped beside me in a car for several hours is an event not likely to occur again. Tentatively I break the silence and ask if this is a good time to discuss some questions about chi kung, and he nods. I ask if the best times to practice chi kung are dawn, noon, twilight and midnight, and he looks at me sideways and asks where I heard this. I tell him I read it in a book, and he says it was a good book then, because these have always been considered the best times to practice, although his own recommendation is different. He says I should practice any time I can, wherever the air is clean.

I ask what direction a person should face when meditating, and he replies south. He adds that it does not matter what hemisphere you are in—south is always the best position to face, and it is also the best direction to point your head when you are sleeping. I remember that his clinic is on a north-south access, and I ask if that was deliberate. He says it was.

In the backseat Tamiyo is rubbing her hands together and asks me to turn up the heat. Tapping Dr. Chow on the shoulder, she asks if a person's chi is weaker in the winter. Dr. Chow speaks to her over his shoulder, saying that chi in a person's body runs strongest in the spring and summer because of the warmer temperatures.

I have read that you should not practice chi kung following sex, or when tired or sick, and I ask Dr. Chow if he agrees with these proscriptions. He shakes his head in disagreement and says one can practice after sex, though the chi will be weaker. He adds that one can certainly practice when tired or sick—in fact, he would recommend it—and also that women can practice while they are menstruating, despite what certain books say to the contrary. He makes these declarations not only as a chi kung master, he says, but as a doctor. Tamiyo asks if there are any times when a person should not practice. Dr. Chow ponders this and then answers that one should not practice after drinking alcohol or when excessively worried. Practicing at such times, he says, can cause the chi to stagnate and that will impede your progress as a student.

Progress! As a chi kung student I know I have made progress, but how much? Unlike the external martial arts with their graded system of colored belts, the internal art of chi kung has no method of gauging progress—other than what the teacher chooses to tell his student, or what the student experiences in his practice. From time to time during the apprenticeship, Dr. Chow informs me when I have reached another level, but the designation is vague, and I would like clarification. What is always understood, but unspoken, is that I must attain a number of levels before I can take the big test. And passing the big test, as I have determined, is a prerequisite to undertaking the arduous training of a chi kung master—at least under this system of apprenticeship.

I turn to Dr. Chow and ask how many levels of mastery there are. He frowns, and I can see him thinking hard in English. Then he speaks, his voice deep in his belly. "No one know."

"No one?"

"Every master say something different. And master who know live on mountain."

"The masters you studied with—who were they?"

Dr. Chow answers, "Had many master." I have asked about his masters because in China the lineage of a chi kung master has always been considered of great importance. To draw him out, I talk about his father, and there is the gleam of memory in his eyes. Of course he learned chi kung from his father, he says. (Why Peter ask question so obvious!) From earlier discussions with the doctor, I know the secrets of chi kung were traditionally passed down from father to son. I am curious to know if he has ever studied with any female chi kung masters, and when I ask him this question he shoots me a quizzical look, half Cheshire cat, half Buddhist sage.

"Why Peter ask this question?" I tell him about a strange dream I had a month ago. In the dream he whispered to me that his grandmother had taught him chi kung. "This good, Peter remember dream."

"Is it true?"

The enigmatic smile returns. "Because no boys in this family, they teach her." His dream-teaching still puzzles me. What if I had not remembered this dream? Would my brain still encode the information somewhere to be retrieved later? And why did he tell me all this in a dream and not in person?

I ask if he will discuss any of his other masters. He says nothing, and I am about to change the subject when he mentions the name Lee Chun-choy, the master who gave him the ling zhi as a parting gift. The specialty of this master, Dr. Chow says, was diseases of the eye. For fourteen years he studied with this master in Shanghai. Along the way, he says, he met many of the doctor's patients, and they never suspected their doctor was also a chi kung master. I look at him askance, and he explains if you announce to the world that you are a chi kung master, people will forever be seeking you out and asking for chi. For someone who seeks a life of tranquility this has little appeal.

From the backseat comes another question from Tamiyo: "The masters who live in the mountains, what are they like?" In a flash Dr. Chow snatches a paper napkin from under the armrest and waves it in the air.

"Here is society," he says, shifting his body toward her. He pokes out two holes and holds the napkin up to his face like a masked bandit in a bad martial arts movie. "Master see through society. He no want. He give up this society, live quiet life in nature. Master live in—" he says the Chinese word, then reverts to English—"Master live in hidden place where no one bother him. Then no one, not even psychic, not even chi kung master, can find him." He lowers the napkin, and his face sinks into repose. I consider the benign face line by line and surmise that he may himself have considered such a life of solitude.

"Did you ever meet such a master?" Tamiyo asks him.

"Did."

"And you studied with him?" she asks. He gives a confirming nod, but does not offer any more. Tamiyo digs further, asking if the master was single or married.

"Married," says Dr. Chow.

"And what did they eat?" she asks.

"Grow vegetable on mountain. And bring herbal medicine from city. I live with them six month."

"Oh, look!" Tamiyo points to a farmer's field where a galloping horse is snorting clouds of steam. Dr. Chow claps his hands with delight. When the moment passes, I turn to him.

"What other masters did you study with, Dr. Chow?" He draws a breath before answering. He says there was a master in Shanghai who did not wish to give out his name. He asked only to be called *Sifu*—master. When Dr. Chow met him, the Sifu was over a hundred years old. The master was stubborn, Dr. Chow says, and prying knowledge out of him was difficult. I ask him if the master is still alive, and Dr. Chow says he thinks so—at least that is his intuition—but after the cultural revolution, the master disappeared. He lapses into a meditative state and then speaks to me in a husky voice. During the cultural revolution, he says, chi kung masters had to go underground. No one could practice openly. Not until the late seventies did the chi kung masters resurface again.

We roll on in silence. After a while I turn on the radio, and some Bourbon Street jazz comes on. Quietly Dr. Chow asks me to turn it off. "Heard this music in Shanghai when I was young."

I turn off the radio. "What kind of music do you like?"

"Chinese opera, some Western classical, and this Fred Astaire—I like his voice." He pauses and picks up the thread of the earlier conversation. "Met this one master at a conference in Shanghai. This master very powerful."

"What was his name?" I ask. Dr. Chow explains that the master had only a nickname—Li Quan—and that he was from the Shandong province. Dr. Chow says he approached the master in the correct manner and asked if he would teach him. The master said he was too busy, but to come back in six months. In the meantime, Dr. Chow says, he tried to find out where the master lived so that he could visit him, but no one knew the master's phone number or address. Six months later he met the master at the appointed time and place, and then the master taught him.

"How long did he teach you?"

"One hour."

"One hour every day?"

"One hour only. And just one day." I think to myself that if ever there are chi kung trading cards, the Li Quan card will be the most sought after, the card with no biographical information on the back. Dr. Chow drops his voice to a confidential whisper. "Can learn many thing in one hour."

"Like what?"

He shakes his head. There is to be no more discussion on this point. Stymied, I change tacks and ask how one approaches a master in the correct manner. Dr. Chow raises his hands above his head and bows down as far as the seatbelt will allow. "To show respect," he says. "Then must give a present—like fruit, money, or maybe clothes. If master accept you, he make teaching schedule. Can be once a month. Never every day." I ask if anyone in North America has ever approached him in the correct manner, and he shoots me a reproving glance. "Peter still have time." Then he slaps his thigh and laughs.

We cross the border into the United States, the lights from passing cars piercing the dusk. Silently we move along a dirt road through frozen pastureland where trees are sinking into the embrace of night. I lower the window to taste the wind, and it is sweet on my tongue. The road of the reservation turns before us, and for miles we follow a twisting ribbon of dirt, past brick houses with cold brick corners until a white-frame house swings into sight.

We alight from the car and cross the pathway, which is powdered with a light snow. Twlya Nitsch, the fabled healer, greets us on the stoop with a kindly smile. She is silver-haired, slender, with a fiery outdoor spirit, but only the high flush of her cheekbones gives a clue as to her native ancestry.

Inside her house she touches a curtain of crystals hanging by the picture window and spends a moment in quiet reflection. She says that Mad Bear—a Cherokee medicine man who lived up the road—just died and that it is a great shame he had not taken on an apprentice because his medicine died with him. She speaks regretfully of the many lost Indian traditions, and then her fiery spirit reasserts itself as she tells us about a young boy who is destined to be a great leader of her people and that she has seen this in his face.

After she makes sure we are comfortable, Twyla fetches questionnaires for us to fill out. From our responses, she says, she will make us each a color chart that will tell us about the hidden traits of our personality. Fifteen minutes later, we hand back the completed questionnaires, and she proceeds to make the charts and then stares open-eyed at the results. "This is remarkable," she says to me. "There are hundreds of possible permutations in a color chart, and yet yours and Dr. Chow's are identical. Both of you have healing as a predominant characteristic; both of you are extremely independent; and both of you have the ability to teach." She goes on for a few minutes like this, and then Dr. Chow says, "Maybe Peter and I have same chart because have same birthday." Now it is my turn to be stunned—the same birthday? I turn to Dr. Chow who throws his head back with a smile. "Of course, Chinese calendar different, birthday change every year."

He reaches over to Twlya and takes her by the hand. "Now I give you gift," he says. They disappear into another room, and moments later I hear Dr. Chow whispering and then Twyla's vibrant voice echoes in the hallway. "The chi! I can feel the chi!" she cries. When they reappear, Dr. Chow is telling Twyla to visit his clinic soon because her internal organs are weak. He makes a generous donation to her teaching center, and we leave.

In the car I ask Dr. Chow about his impression of Twyla. "Lovely woman, have power, but internal organ weak. Need some medicine." (Subsequent to our visit, Twyla made two trips to the clinic, and we greeted each other like old friends in the waiting room. But on her second trip she told me the long drive was too much for her and she would not be coming back.)

A mile from the border we make a stop at the duty-free store, and for a lark I buy a phone in the shape of an apple. At the border crossing a customs officer sticks his head in the driver's window.

"How long you folks been out of Canada?"

"A few hours," I say.

"Buy anything?" I hold up the apple-phone. The eyes of the customs officer flash with victory, and he says I have not been out of the country long enough to claim an exemption. He points to a building and tells me to pull over. Inside the building the three of us approach the counter, Dr. Chow with confidence, and I with its jangly counterfeit. A small gray man behind the counter produces a triplicate form and asks for my driver's license. As I fish out my wallet, Dr. Chow speaks to him in a soft low voice.

"Peter don't know pay this duty. Maybe this time you let go with warning."

The man pays no attention and begins filling out the triplicate form, then ups his head and looks at me. "This your current address?"

Before I can answer, Dr. Chow massages the air with his fingers in the direction of the small gray man. "Peter didn't know pay this duty," he says. "Maybe this time let go with warning." For a brief moment the small gray man appears frozen, his pen suspended above the triplicate form. Dr. Chow continues to stroke the air with his fingers. "So maybe just let go." With a jerk the small gray man comes to life. He places his pen on the counter and gives me an admonishing look.

"You should have known the rules," he says. "But you didn't, so I'm going to let you off with a warning this time. Have a good trip." I glance at Tamiyo whose mouth is hanging open. Dr. Chow guides us to the door, then spins around and gives a wave to the small gray man.

"Thank you," says the doctor with a smile. Disoriented, the small gray man turns away.

In the car I gaze at the road ahead, lost in amazement. After a moment I turn to Dr. Chow and thank him for his beau geste. I tell him the masters he studied under must have been formidable. "Peter," he says with a shy smile as if to imply he has done nothing. We continue up the highway under a full witch's moon. I glance at Tamiyo in the rearview mirror.

"Obi Wan Kenobi from *Star Wars*," she says with wide unblinking eyes. "Dr. Chow is a Jedi knight."

Clever Men

It's Sunday afternoon, and Dr. Chow is ensconced in his office. I have come to collect him for a small get-together, but he is waiting for a phone call, and so I drop myself in the patient's chair and rest my elbows on the desk. In my hand I have a book called *Living Magic*, written by a parapsychologist named Ronald Rose. The book, published in 1956, is a treasure trove of the magical practices of Australian Aborigines, practices that survived for thousands of years and now have all but vanished. While Dr. Chow waits for his call, I show him a photograph in the book of a naked Aborigine. The Aborigine glowers at the camera with fierce determination.

"He's a chi kung master," I say, "but in Australia they call their chi kung masters 'clever men.'"

"Clever men," he says, rolling the words around in his mouth. He turns the page and bends towards another photograph. He taps his fingernail at a strange object in the corner, and I tell him he is looking at a small piece of human bone that is attached to a length of human hair. The Aborigines call it a pointing bone, I tell him. If a clever man points the bone at you, you die. Up shoots the doctor's head. "This work if you believe in it," he says.

"Yes, they call it a spear of thought. But they say the best clever men can make it work regardless of belief. They say they can point the bone at you when you are not looking, and the result is the same." He gives no response. I remind him of the wand he "charged up" for me. I make the case that a chi kung master could put killing energy in a wand instead of healing energy. Dr. Chow agrees without a ripple of expression on his face. "Then why not with a pointing bone?" I ask.

He sits still for a moment, and I am conscious of the silence. Then he speaks in a low undertone. "Chi kung master don't need this bone or this wand. Can throw chi into your body and make your organs very sick. No doctor can heal you then."

It is a strange conversation to be having on a Sunday afternoon, or on any afternoon for that matter. Dr. Chow goes on to say that a person who understands how to manipulate energy can leave a package of chi behind at any designated place. The next person who visits that place will absorb the chi—whether that chi be beneficial or harmful. But a chi kung master would never injure someone, he quickly adds.

"Chi kung master must have—" he switches to Chinese, then gives the translation—"must have kind heart." It occurs to me that the phenomenon of chi being left behind must also happen involuntarily—hence the notion of good and bad vibes that people feel at any particular place. I ask him if he has ever known a master with bad vibes. Not a chi kung master, he says, but there are other kinds of masters—shamanic practitioners—who can hurt you or steal your chi.

I ask him how someone knows when his chi has been stolen, and he says novice students do not know—they only feel tired. But chi kung masters can always tell if their chi is stolen, he says. They can feel someone steal their chi, and they can also see when chi leaves their body. Of course, masters can protect themselves, he says, by closing their chakras. He glances at his watch. "Sorry, waiting so long for phone call."

I show him other photographs in the book. One is of an Aboriginal clever man reputed to travel vast distances in the twinkling of any eye. I ask if chi kung masters can do the same thing. Dr. Chow has his gaze fixed on the phone. He stares at it so intently I expect the receiver to levitate into his hand. "Beg a pardon?" he says, turning toward me. I repeat the question, and his brow grows thoughtful. "In chi kung, not travel fast this way. Travel fast another way."

"Which way is that?"

He leans back in his chair and sinks into rumination. With a gaze that looks far beyond me, he recounts a story that took place in Peking at the turn of the 19th century. A famous chi kung doctor was attending a banquet held in his honor, when into the banquet hall rushed a messenger, shouting to the assembled guests: "A patient is very ill and needs the doctor!" Everyone was upset that the doctor might have to leave, because so much trouble had gone into the banquet preparations. But the doctor kept eating and did not leave. Dr. Chow opens his mouth and feigns eating a variety of dishes with imaginary chopsticks. Evidently the master in this story was sumptuously fed.

"Why didn't the doctor attend to the patient and then return to the banquet?" Dr. Chow draws a breath and explains that the patient lived on the opposite side of the city, quite a distance by rickshaw. But the doctor knew he had to do something, as the patient was in dire straits. Imitating the patient, Dr. Chow turns his face ashen, and makes his eyes dull and lifeless. He looks truly ill, and for a moment I am alarmed. Then he straightens his posture, and the color floods back into his face.

"So what to do?" he says. "Doctor must see patient! So—doctor see patient!"

"But I thought the doctor didn't leave the banquet."

"Didn't leave." He brings his face closer to mine. "But still he see patient." I ask how the doctor could be in two places at the same time, and Dr. Chow lifts his eyebrows and lets his hands flutter in opposite directions.

"Chi kung," he says.

"Perhaps the doctor was projecting his astral body at the banquet," I say to Dr. Chow. "In other words, he wasn't there in physical form, but in a kind of spirit form."

"No, he eat and drink. Have body."

"Then perhaps he was using his astral body to appear before the patient."

"No, he use needles on this patient."

"Perhaps the doctor had a twin or a brother or a cousin who resembled him."

"No, didn't have."

"Perhaps the people at the banquet were hypnotized and only thought that he was there."

"This possible," he says. "But don't think so."

I remember that Carlos Castaneda wrote about the phenomenon of the double in his book *Tales of Power*. Carlos's teacher, Don Juan, said the double was as real as it could be and was arrived at by dreaming. But when Carlos pressed Don Juan for concrete examples of how real the double was, Don Juan was evasive in his response. I remember thinking at the time that the double might be a strong astral projection, capable of limited physical acts, but not a separate physical body. Of course, many people have stated that Don Juan himself never even existed, or was a composite figure, drawn from the many healers Castaneda had known.

I regard Dr. Chow intently. "Do you really think a chi kung master can split himself into two bodies?" He strokes his chin. In chi kung lore, he says, there are many stories like this, and there is even a special word to describe this phenomenon. He writes down the ideogram and pushes it toward me. The ideogram translates as "split-body chi kung."

Now he lowers his voice. "But split-body chi kung very hard. Only for emergency. Only for—how you say—clever men." The phone rings with mysterious promise, and he answers it, exchanges some breathless talk in Chinese, hangs up, and thrusts himself to his feet. "We go now. But must come back, two hours. Must see this patient."

We hurry out of the clinic. Dr. Chow has never before seen my red sportscar—a 1955 Austin-Healey—and is delighted by the primitive instrument cluster. I explain that despite the cooling weather, we will be riding with the top down because the undercarriage of the top is broken. Dr. Chow glances upward, and for a moment his face shows concern. The clouds, banked high, are darkening.

My car, a two-seater, is built low to the ground, but the doctor slides into the passenger seat with ease and gropes about for a seatbelt until I inform him that no seatbelt exists. He braces his knees on either side of the passenger compartment and grips the chrome handle attached to the dashboard. "Okay, ready, go!" he says.

I pull out the choke and touch the electric starter button, and the engine shakes boisterously. In five seconds we are roaring along the street with the wind streaming through our hair. From the expression on his face I can tell Dr. Chow loves the open feeling of the car. Everything we pass is of interest to him, and his glance roves wildly. As his excitement rises, so does my cornering speed, and he laughs and pounds the dashboard with glee. I almost ask him if his pounding fist has transferred chi into the car and what that would mean, but instead I flip the overdrive switch and press on the accelerator. Dr. Chow bounces up and down with excitement, which is partly owing to the bad suspension of the car.

The early models of the Austin-Healey come with no radio, and we drive in silent communion for a few miles, the engine heat keeping us warm as the cool wind smacks against our foreheads. Suddenly the doctor breaks out: "What they want me talk about at this party?" I can tell from his voice that he does not wish to figure largely at this party, if he must figure at all.

"You can talk about whatever you want, Dr. Chow. It's just a collection of people who want to discuss energy." I remind him that two of his patients are hosting the party—Ted Mann and his wife Diane.

Building after building floats by. Then the city spins away entirely, and we find ourselves on a long curving road that leads us through a suburban neighborhood of wide lawns and well-built houses. The houses blur together until they resolve into a single dwelling, and suddenly we have arrived. A spitting rain has begun, and we jump out of the car, secure the tonneau cover over the seats, and run to the porch where we shake off the drops like dogs.

Among the guests assembled by Ted and Diane are a physicist, an electrical engineer, a woman who has studied with a Cree shaman, and a Reiki practitioner. During the discussion Dr. Chow speaks very little, but lends an avid ear. At one point the electrical engineer directs a question to him, inquiring if standing chi kung is more powerful than sitting chi kung, and Dr. Chow allows that it is. In standing chi kung, the doctor says, less chi is lost to the external world. He adds that in the standing posture, chi escapes only from the practitioner's feet, whereas in the sitting posture chi is lost to the chair as well as the floor.

The physicist then asks if a chi kung practitioner could stand with one foot off the ground to minimize the loss of chi. Dr. Chow says it is possible and that some yogis in India practice this way, but "this not elegant." Not elegant—the personality of the ballroom dancer has surfaced. The rain continues unabated, and Ted Mann remarks how unfortunate it is that Wilhelm Reich is not still alive. Ted reminds the group that Reich believed people could control the weather with their orgone energy.

An hour into the gathering, Dr. Chow begins to shift around in his chair. The rain shows no signs of letting up, and I begin to contemplate how we will make it back in the open car. With an almost imperceptible nod of his head, Dr. Chow indicates to me that he is ready to leave. Just at that moment his wrist is caught by the woman who studied with a Cree shaman. She takes the chair beside him, and Dr. Chow's wonderful manners keep him sitting beside her, as he crinkles his eyes in an effort of amiability.

"You're really a chi kung master?" she asks.

"Am."

Her face is rapt. "I want to know if a chi kung master can push another person away without any physical contact."

The doctor's eyes become pensive. "This depend on power of master, and energy system of other person."

"Is it easier to push the body of a student who has trained with you?" she asks. "I've heard that a master can make his student fly like a kite for several seconds." The expression "fly like a kite" mystifies Dr. Chow, and the woman has to explain what it means. A pause follows, then he says, "If student is beginner, then have no chakras open, then this more difficult for master to make fly like kite. If student more advanced, have chakras open, then this much easier. But advanced student also can close chakras and make this difficult. But I no make student fly like kite. Might fly Peter through window by mistake."

He gives a laugh to indicate he has made a joke, then springs to his feet and, moving with consummate ease, says his goodbyes to everyone, shaking their hands and releasing little bursts of chi into their palms. If the guests notice any energy exchange, they never comment. But suddenly they all begin asking him questions, to which Dr. Chow smilingly responds, "Sorry, must see patient!" With his arm outstretched, he makes for the door. Ted

Mann has given me two umbrellas to hold over our heads for our drive, but when I look out the window, I see the rain has suddenly stopped, the sky pouring a bright light on the road.

As Dr. Chow and I speed home in the open car, I mention the book on Aborigines again. "The clever men say they can control the weather."

"Isn't it?" he says.

"In chi kung, same thing?"

A long pause. "Can."

"The clever men use spirits to do this."

He turns his head very slightly toward me. "Not this way in chi kung. Use chi."

"Is it very hard to do, Dr. Chow?"

The doctor deliberates for a moment, then without looking at me, drops his voice. "Weather very hard influence. More hard than fly a student like kite, more hard than influence animal, than influence plant, even than influence object."

The makers of the 1955 Austin-Healey designed an adjustable windshield that can be lowered below the level of the steering wheel, and the feeling is like riding a motorcycle without a helmet. At a stoplight, I lower the windshield, and then we speed toward the tilting sky, a fresh-scented silence washing over our faces.

Out of a Misty Dream

Dr. Chow needs herbs for a patient, rare herbs that he does not have at the clinic, so I am ferrying him to Chinatown in my car. After today I will not see him for two weeks because in the evening he will board a plane for China. We reach the herbalist store, and I tell him I will wait. But he says for me to go on, that he has many things to do in Chinatown. Before stepping out of the car he grips my left wrist, and a dart of chi flies up my arm to my heart.

"Get ready," he says.

"Get ready for what?"

"Big test." The two words strike my whole being with a nervous delight. If Dr. Chow had taken my pulse at that very moment, its rapidity would have alarmed him. A legion of acupuncture needles could not have slowed its manic rhythm. He is out of the car now, and I call after him through the window.

"What should I do to prepare myself?" Even to my pounding ears the question sounds superfluous.

"Pay attention!" he cries and glides away.

One of the paradoxes of not being able to prepare for an uncertain situation of great consequence is that the mind and body leap into a state of high alert. Recently I have been writing episodes of *Tintin* for HBO, episodes based on the French comic books, and the investigating zeal of the teenage detective now overtakes my own personality. For the rest of the day I am on the lookout for anything unusual. My detective work, though, is directed not to the external world, but to the world roiling inside me. For hours on end my mind observes every racing thought and magnifies every bodily sensation, lest some clue to the big test arrive by stealth. Come nightfall I am spent. I can no longer feel, think, imagine. I decide to practice chi kung in bed, but the moment I crawl under the covers, I fall asleep. And then I have a dream.

In the dream Dr. Chow is on a plane, and he is telling me he will throw chi to me at 1:30, and that I must remember this conversation. Waking up, I remember thinking that he did not specify whether he was throwing chi at 1:30 a.m, 1:30 p.m., or 1:30 according to the time in China.

The next day I am in a state of elation. I have completed the first part of the big test, which is to discover the nature of the test itself. The dream occupies all my thoughts, and at lunch with a friend, I keep glancing surreptitiously at my watch—1:30, 1:45, 2:00. Was my chi too weak to catch Dr. Chow's throw? Was his throw too faint to make an impression? Or was this the wrong time for the throw?

It is now Saturday morning, two days have passed since the dream, and I have not experienced any transmission of chi. I plunge into despair as I recall the first conversation I ever had with Dr. Chow about the big test. *But what if I don't pass the big test? What happens then?*

Apprenticeship ends. You leave the clinic.

A few hours later I am watching television with a downcast face when suddenly I feel a detonation of chi at the base of my spine. I spring from my chair and check my watch. The time of the throw is 1:23 p.m. Immediately the chi diffuses through my body, and I can feel its presence for a long time thereafter.

The day Dr. Chow returns from China, I pay a visit to his office. He looks like he has not slept for a long time, but his dark eyes are still bright. Leaning in the doorway, my heart beating quickly, I tell him I had a dream about the big test and the time of his throw, but in the dream he did not specify what day the test was to take place. His face gives away nothing. "What day I throw it?"

"Saturday," I reply.

He sits up straight with sudden alertness. "What time I throw it?" he asks.

"I dreamed you were going to throw it at 1:30," I say. "But you threw it earlier."

"Oh, this about 1:20, 1:25," he says. "I start little early, make sure you get it."

He gestures to the patient's chair, and I sit down. A torrent of talk comes next as he describes his trip, the patients he met, the food he ate, the friends he visited. The recollection illumines his eyes, and he gives swift sketches of modern life in Shanghai, a city unrecognizable from the city of his youth. But I am scarcely listening to a word he says. I am still rejoicing in my moment of triumph. When he has finished talking, he locks his fingers together and fixes me with his gaze. "What else did Peter notice?"

I have been expecting this question. I tell him I recorded four other throws after the one on Saturday. As I begin to reel off the times and varying intensity of each throw, Dr. Chow tears his locked fingers apart and shouts: "Peter pass big test!" I laugh with a relief mingled with pure pleasure.

"So what happens next, Dr. Chow?"

"We let chi decide," he says in a tone of great gentleness. "Chi know best."

The Offer

"What you really want?" Dr. Chow is looking at me with a searching wonder. He spreads his hands wide upon the desk, indicating it would please rather than perturb him if I asked to learn the entire encyclopedia of his knowledge. Before I can even take a breath, he adds, "And later, can open your own clinic."

There is a great humming sound in my ears. In my mind I flash through snapshots of smiling patients, an acupuncture needle pinched between thumb and forefinger, a white lab coat draped on my frame, a warren of examination rooms, an office, a large appointment book, the drifting scent of pungent herbs, Chinese medical texts—I will learn Chinese!—the swells and falls of Mozart in the hallway, and everywhere the all-pervading chi. Two seconds, and it is over.

Perhaps it is an adverse star that keeps me from seizing what might be the greatest opportunity of my life. But I know it is not in my nature to run an acupuncture clinic five days a week, let alone spend the years required to master the craft. Nor is my interest in Chinese herbs of a sufficient level to make me want to devote the requisite years of study. Only chi, with its infinitude of mystery, can hold my continued interest for a lifetime of learning.

I look at the doctor without speaking, considering how I can disengage myself from his grand scheme. Previously he stated he would never pull me away from my writing. Once when I was being considered for the job of head writer for a television series, he wished me luck and said he would continue the apprenticeship if I got the job. I did not get the job and was disappointed, but back in the clinic I received such a smattering of chi that the world righted itself almost immediately. For years the doctor has shown a paternal interest in my writing career and even, at one point, introduced me to a film producer who was a patient. But here I am, sitting before him in his office, and he is suggesting— no, advocating—that I embark on a career in traditional Chinese medicine. I am aware that his brother Alan recently left to start his own practice. There is a void in the clinic that needs to be filled. But right now I am at a loss for words.

His eyes are scrutinizing me. After a moment's vivid pause, he speaks. "You have a fear. A fear of death. Of patients dying." My heart twists; he is right. I once considered what it would be like to have my own clinic, and I realized I could never forgive myself if someone died in my care.

Finally I speak. "I don't see myself running a clinic, Dr. Chow, but I can see myself writing and speaking about chi kung. And I will do other things as well. I can't do just one thing."

He gives a laugh of perceptive sympathy. "Of course, this your nature. This the nature of your chi." The phone rings. A patient is calling from Hong Kong. Dr. Chow gives me a small wave, and from his fingertips comes a scattershot of chi that hits my body at different points simultaneously. The meeting is over. The chi has decided. The chi knows best.

Goodbye, But not Farewell

When you are a writer, and you are living with an actress, the city of Los Angeles will call to you at some point. You will either heed the call, or you will tell yourself that where you are living is a fine enough place, that the change of seasons is something you look forward to every year, that the cold of winter is something you can endure (for you have endured it these many years), that if the lowering sky ever crashes too close to your head, why you can always take a vacation to some warm place.

On a day of record-breaking chill I stand in the doorway of Dr. Chow's office and tell him of my plan to move to Los Angeles. He listens courteously and when I finish my little speech, he wishes me well. My announcement comes as no surprise to him, I think. Has he not seen this coming for some time? *Peter like these palm tree more than he know.*

"Should come back whenever you can, continue your training," he says. "There is more to learn." I tell him I will come back frequently, and then I ask what he thinks of me teaching chi kung privately in Los Angeles. He says it is a good idea, and it could benefit people. He reminds me of the stationary postures he has taught me as well as the different sets of moving exercises.

"And I thought I might do some healings as well," I tell him.

He shakes his head in a disapproving way. "Not like this."

"Why not?"

"Your chi get low fast."

"But I know how to replenish my chi."

"This true," he says, "but better you build up your body. If throw chi now, stay at same level in your practice or get weaker. Must develop more power." As he speaks, my right leg begins tingling.

"Where are you throwing the chi from?" I ask. He waggles his right foot under the desk.

"From your foot?" I ask incredulously.

"Big toe," he says, under the normal key of his voice and then laughs.

"Where else can you throw it from?"

"From any chi kung point in my body." He indicates the major points on his back, head, neck, chest, arms, legs, hands, and feet.

"What about regular acupuncture points? Can you throw chi from those as well?"

"Can," he says, "but these points not so strong, energy not so concentrated."

He sags back in his chair and looks at me. "Remember when you first felt the chi?"

I remember distinctly, and I describe to him the feeling. "And I almost didn't become your apprentice," I say, "because after the first two courses, I could feel the chi in my body even when I wasn't practicing. I would lie on the couch and watch television and feel chi flowing through me. So I thought to myself, why study any more?" He says nothing in return, but something in his eyes make me reflect upon my memory, and suddenly it all becomes clear. "You were throwing chi to me then. That's why I felt it so strongly." He lets a smile form on his lips. "So when did my apprenticeship really begin?" I ask.

"First day you studied chi kung with me." He says nothing, but sits silent, as do I, in the stillness of the room. From the silence and stillness comes serenity, and it is profound and all around us until I speak again. I tell him I plan to write a book about my experiences. I paraphrase a passage from *The Yellow Emperor's Classic of Internal Medicine*: "One should make public upon tablets of jade that which was hidden and concealed and thus make known the precious mechanism of the universe."

Dr. Chow smiles in recognition of the words, and then says I should use my Chinese brain when I write the book. I say I will gladly use any brain in my head that is functioning. Choosing what to include is the difficult part, I add. He replies that I should tell less rather than more. A woman clothed is more interesting than a woman naked, he says.

I have no memory of our leave-taking that day. Probably the doctor gave me some chi as a parting gift, but my mind, my body, do not recall. Already my thoughts had flown to the great adventure that lay ahead in California. The ancient mystery of chi, I would carry with me, reposing my trust in its corrective power, observing through its movements the deeper reality that lies beyond appearances.

About the Author

PETER MEECH was born in Toronto and received a Master's degree in communications from Stanford University where he won a Nicol fellowship for writing.

Peter has served as a script doctor on several feature films and has written for a variety of television shows, including Robert Halmi's *Dracula: the Series* (syndicated), *Ready or Not* (Showtime), *Tintin* (HBO), *Masked Rider* (Fox Family), *VR Troopers* (Fox Family) and *Emily of New Moon* (Disney, CBC). Peter has written for German television and has also worked in Japan, producing a Japanese movie, *Jenifa*, with Robbie Robertson, starring Takayuki Yamada and Jennifer Holmes.

He is a member of the Animation Caucus of the Writer's Guild of America, the Writer's Guild of Canada, the British Academy of Film and Television, and the Screen Actor's Guild.

Peter divides his time between Toronto and Los Angeles.

Sentient Publications, LLC publishes books on cultural creativity, experimental education, transformative spirituality, holistic health, new science, ecology, and other topics, approached from an integral viewpoint. Our authors are intensely interested in exploring the nature of life from fresh perspectives, addressing life's great questions, and fostering the full expression of the human potential. Sentient Publications' books arise from the spirit of inquiry and the richness of the inherent dialogue between writer and reader.

Our Culture Tools series is designed to give social catalyzers and cultural entrepreneurs the essential information, technology, and inspiration to forge a sustainable, creative, and compassionate world.

We are very interested in hearing from our readers. To direct suggestions or comments to us, or to be added to our mailing list, please contact:

SENTIENT PUBLICATIONS, LLC
1113 Spruce Street
Boulder, CO 80302
303-443-2188
contact@sentientpublications.com
www.sentientpublications.com